AME
SHORT STORIES

Edited by Barry Taylor

Illustrated by Clyde Pearson

Longman

Longman Group UK Limited
Longman House, Burnt Mill, Harlow,
Essex CM20 2JE, England
and Associated Companies throughout the world.

This edition © Longman Group Ltd 1964

*First published *1964*
Nineteenth impression 1988

Produced by Longman Group (FE) Ltd
Printed in Hong Kong

ISBN 0-582-53026-1

THE BRIDGE SERIES

The *Bridge Series* is intended for students of English as a second or foreign language who have progressed beyond the elementary graded readers and the *Longman Simplified English Series* but are not yet sufficiently advanced to read works of literature in their original form.

The books in the *Bridge Series* are moderately simplified in vocabulary and often slightly reduced in length, but with little change in syntax. The purpose of the texts is to give practice in understanding fairly advanced sentence patterns and to help in the appreciation of English style. We hope that they will prove enjoyable to read for their own sake and that they will at the same time help students to reach the final objective of reading original works of literature in English with full understanding and appreciation.

Technical Note

The vocabulary of the *Simplified English Series* is the 2,000 words of the *General Service List* (*Interim Report on Vocabulary Selection*) and there is a degree of structure control. In the *Bridge Series* words outside the commonest 7,000 (in Thorndike and Lorge: *A Teacher's Handbook of 30,000 Words*, Columbia University, 1944) have usually been replaced by commoner and more generally useful words. Words used which are outside the first 3,000 of the list are explained in a glossary and are so distributed throughout the book that they do not occur at a greater density than 25 per running 1,000 words.

THE AMERICAN SHORT STORY

A short story is a tale that can be read aloud in half an hour or so, the result, as has been said, of a sudden passion. As its title suggests, it is the kind of story that must concentrate on one event and one main character to make an effect upon the reader. This does not mean that the story is less important than a longer novel. But it does mean that to be successful the author must know precisely what it is he wants to write about and exactly how to write it. This is the challenge of the short story.

The first successful American short stories came from Washington Irving about eighteen hundred and twenty. But it is Edgar Allan Poe who is generally thought of as the true beginner because he gave shape and plan to his mysterious tales. He was followed by Hawthorne who brought ideas to this form of art, giving the reader more to think about.

It was Bret Harte in his tales from California who finally made the short story seem completely at home in the United States. Here at last were characters who were American and could be nothing else. At the end of the century Henry James brought to the form a careful writing that has made his stories models of their art.

In the twentieth century, besides the writers found in this book, there have been many who have won fame abroad as well as in the United States for their stories. The most remarkable is certainly William Faulkner whose description of the southern states has helped towards a more honest understanding of the people who live there. And for those who like to be more up-to-date still, J. D. Salinger and John Updike are only two of the writers who are now making sure that the American short story continues to be read— because of its excellence and variety.

CONTENTS

ACKNOWLEDGEMENTS

We are grateful to the following for permission to include copyright material:

Constable & Co. Ltd. and J. B. Lippincott Co. for 'A Piece of Pie' from *Guys and Dolls* by Damon Runyon, published by J. B. Lippincott Co. under the title *Take It Easy*, copyright 1937 by Damon Runyon; the Executors of the Ernest Hemingway Estate for 'The Killers' from *Great Men and Women* by Ernest Hemingway, published by Jonathan Cape Ltd.; *The New Yorker* for 'The Night the Ghost Got In' by James Thurber, copyright 1933 and 1961 The New Yorker Magazine Inc.; and the author's agents and Harold Matson Co. Inc. for 'Out of the Past' from *The Pioneers* by Jack Schaefer, copyright 1954 by Jack Schaefer.

Out of the Past

JACK SCHAEFER

Jack Schaefer (1907–), like many American writers, began his career as a journalist. Some years after the Second World War he started writing novels, many of them about the West of the United States and the Red Indian wars of one hundred years ago. His first novel *Shane* was a great success and was made into an equally successful film. All his stories are about simple direct people—farmers, settlers, miners, soldiers. Naturally enough, they are concerned with action rather than thinking, and the following story, which is really three stories for the price of one, is a representative example.

THIS is a story of revenge. But revenge is an ugly word. It carries suggestions of hatred and personal viciousness that may or may not be involved. There are times when revenge is more accurately a plain balancing of accounts, an expression of one man's loyalty to another. It is a balancing of accounts, an expression of loyalty bridging many miles and many years, that is told here.

This is a story, too, of three parts. Three happenings. Three individual bursts of violent action separated in time and place. I will not tell you whether these happenings were true in actual fact. That is no longer important at this date. But you should know that they could have been true. Such things happened in this America in the years of westward settlement. I will not even insist that you accept these three happenings as parts of the one same story. I am content to present them as you might come upon them searching, as I have often done, through the records of that westward settlement, the old letters and books and newspapers that remain as a legacy to us out of the past.

First, a letter. A letter written from a military post in the dry badlands of southern New Mexico in 1885.

This letter was written by a soldier, a sergeant, a cavalry-man, to his mother back home in Missouri. He wrote it lying on a bed in a curtained-off section of a mud and log-walled barracks marked with a sign that said 'Hospital'. He was a badly wounded, badly shaken man, deeply grateful that he was alive and that he would live. The tone of his letter and a few hints in the text suggest that he was young without being youthful, maybe in his middle twenties, reasonably well educated for the time and the territory, a serious, capable man and a good soldier. He wrote the letter in parts on several different days, probably because he was too weak to do it all at once. His story of what had happened is rambling and understandably confused but the main outline is clear and direct.

Geronimo was off the reservation again, he and his Apaches[1] off on their last and bitterest raiding war. Troops were out after them and this soldier, this sergeant, was with those troops. The Apaches were up to their usual trick of scattering to strike in many places at the same time and the troops were spread thin in small groups searching the territory. The detachment this sergeant was with had penetrated some rough country. The enemy were near. The Indian guide leading the way slowed down till the horses were barely moving and said the signs spoke trouble. The lieutenant in command had the sense to guess that was warning enough and called a halt where rocks gave good cover in case of an attack. He sent the sergeant and the Indian guide on forward. There was no way of knowing whether the Apaches in the area had seen the detachment yet. The plan was for those two to look over the ground ahead and try to find the enemy, if possible without being seen. They were to go maybe three miles but no farther. If nothing developed they were to look for another easily defended spot and one of them slip back to bring up the full detachment. The lieutenant was a cautious man, a good officer. He was going to move now only from strong position to strong position, not risking his whole command in a possible ambush.

[1] Apaches: Red Indian tribesmen of the United States.

That's the picture to hold in mind. Two men riding forward. Two men obeying orders and riding forward into rough country with the enemy close about them. One of them is the sergeant, the letter writer, a good soldier who is serious about the army as a career and has won his promotion early in the army. The other is an Indian, a Miniconjou Sioux from the northern plains, a man well into middle age who has fought the white men in the strength of his youth and seen his tribe dwindle in defeat and has wandered far and has served now several years as a guide with the men he once fought. It is the Indian who emerges in fairly clear focus, seen as the sergeant saw him, not to the sergeant just an Indian hidden by his race, in which all seem the same because of their very difference, but a man distinct and individual with the marks of a hard life upon him. He is a man of medium height, thick in the body with shoulders not wide but thick all through and a heaviness around the hips. His eyes are small and black in a flat face full of old small-pox scars and he limps with his right leg from a stiffness in the knee and two fingers of his left hand are missing. He is a man hidden behind the blank wall of his flat expressionless face, nothing to look at in old Army trousers and shirt faded past colour, yet a man on whose word an experienced lieutenant would set the safety of his command and not think twice about it.

They rode forward. They went cautiously, keeping in cover, working their way upwards as the land rose towards a long ridge across their course. They stopped. Ahead and beyond the ridge they saw a thin stream of smoke floating upward. A signal? A campfire? They moved forward again, even more slowly. They dropped into a gully that led towards the ridge top. The Indian was in the lead, head up, eyes alert, ready for anything. Suddenly he turned his horse and waved to the sergeant to do the same and drove back down the gully at full gallop. As he passed the sergeant in the act of swinging his horse, the first shots came from up the gully among rocks along the sides. A bullet went through the sergeant's left leg above the knee and into his horse and the horse went down and he was thrown off and rolled headlong, striking against a stone that made an ugly wound along his jaw, and as he

3

rolled in the turning he saw the Indian guide disappearing down the gully and then the Apaches scrambling out from among the rocks up the gully and starting towards him. He did not know where his rifle was. It had fallen from his grasp and lay somewhere beyond the dying horse. He could not stand but he pushed up, leaning on his left arm, and got at his revolver and had it in his right hand when another bullet hit his shoulder and he was flat and helpless on the ground.

Curiously he felt no pain in the shock of that moment. But everything about him was remarkably clear and distinct, the hard ground beneath and the clear hot blue of the sky overhead and beyond and above all else the complete aloneness. He could hear the shouts of the Apaches coming and somehow the sounds did not penetrate the silence that surrounded him. And into that silence and that aloneness came another sound that could penetrate and that hit him as even the bullets had not. It was the sound of hoofs and he could move and raise his head and twist it to look back down the gully. The Indian guide had turned his horse again and was racing towards him, low-bent over the horse's neck, reaching with one arm to beat the frightened animal to greater speed. The Indian guide pulled the horse to a stop by the sergeant and jumped off and picked up the sergeant like a soft sack of grain and threw him over the horse and jumped again into the saddle and the animal struggled into a gallop beneath the double burden.

How long they rode that way the sergeant could not know. The beating of the horse under him was a dreadful torment. He had time only to think that it was hopeless, that this horse was carrying double and the Apaches would have their own horses hidden near and be after them and overtake them, and then the shaking was too much and he dropped into darkness.

That was early afternoon. It was late afternoon when he regained consciousness for a few moments. He was lying in a tight hole between two big rocks. All he could see was the stone sides rising and the patch of deepening blue of sky between. Then he was aware that an Indian with a flat scarred face, naked to the waist, was bandaging or rebandaging his shoulder with pieces of a

4

faded old Army shirt. Again he had time for only one thought. He was thinking that this Indian was doing a good job, considering the fact that two fingers of his left hand were missing, when the darkness rose and overcame him. Much later his mind came back for a few seconds out of that darkness into another, into the darkness of the moonless starry night, and he was aware that he was being carried, lying limp and bent over the thick shoulder and upper arm of a man. He could hear the slow strained breathing of the man carrying him and then he knew nothing and then drops of some raw stuff, rum or whisky, were going down his throat and he was lying on the ground about thirty feet from a small fire and the lieutenant was kneeling beside him. He tried to move and sit up, fighting the pain that ran through his stiffened body, and the lieutenant pushed him to the ground. 'Easy,' the lieutenant said. 'You're not going anywhere. There's a lot of them out there. They've got us pinned down tight.' And still the sergeant tried to move, to turn his head and look about, and the lieutenant understood. 'He waited till dark to bring you in. But he's gone now. He slipped out again to try for reinforcements.'

There it is, all that is needed. The rest of the letter is unimportant. What it tells is, in a sense, anticlimax. Reinforcements came and the Apaches sighted them and faded farther into the badlands. The sergeant and two other wounded were sent back in a wagon. He was out of the war, out of the long later days of fighting and hard riding and knew only by hearsay what those days brought. He was on a hospital bed with two bullet wounds which the doctor said would heal nicely and with a hole in the side of his jaw which the doctor said would leave a neat scar to remind him of what he had been through.

Lying there, writing his letter, this sergeant had plenty of time to think over what he could remember of what had happened and to wonder what must have happened during the hours he was lost in the darkness and an ageing Indian with a limping leg got him away from Geronimo's Apaches and took him through to the safety of the detachment's rock defences. That impressed him deeply and he wrote about it at length. But what impressed him more was the sudden breaking of his aloneness as he lay helpless on the ground in the gully. His mind returned to that again and again. Three times the same brief sentence jumps out of the letter. HE CAME BACK.

Second, an account of a court trial in a paper-bound local history of a Kansas town. The trial occurred in 1898. That is a jump of thirteen years in time and several hundred miles north-westward in place. But the mind can make it in an instant if interest holds.

This trial is quoted in the town history as an example of the long lasting frontier conditions, of the kind of excitement that could still break out in that part of Kansas near the turn of the century. The historian himself offers no hint of his sympathies in the case. He simply offers the facts established by the evidence and makes a summary of the testimony taken. Out of these facts and the testimony comes a plain picture of the event at issue and the reasons for the verdict given.

Background is important here. The town was close to an Army post, a cavalry headquarters and supply depot. Some people liked that, those who made money out of the soldiers, especially during the first week after each pay-day. Other people didn't like it, those with short memories who could forget the time when the presence of troops was a comfort for settlers, and those compelled by the need to impose their type of respectability on their fellows. There were complaints from time to time about fighting and noisy disturbances in the saloons and the unavoidable collection of rough and often unpleasant individuals who collected in the neighbourhood of an Army camp. A particular annoyance to many people seems to have been a small number of Indians, most of them fairly old in years, who lived near the post with the apparent permission of the commanding officer and wandered in and out of the town with no visible means of support.

That was the situation when a sudden change took place. Far off in Havana harbour the battleship MAINE was sunk. The United States declared war on Spain. The troops at this Kansas post were ordered east to Cuba. Within ten days the post was deserted except for a small group left to take it to pieces. An unnatural quiet settled over the outlying section of the town that had annoyed so many respectable citizens. And out of that quiet came the sudden violence that caused the trial.

The key character was a bartender, a reckless, red-headed talkative man. He must have had a quick temper to go with the hair and the touch of cruelty in him, because his wife had left him and had been trying to divorce him on precisely those grounds. Yet he was well liked in the district, among the men at least, well enough for some of them to lend a few dollars each and pay his lawyer when he was brought to trial. And apparently he was good at his job. His employer had kept him on month after month even though he was constantly exceeding his pay. It was a better than average bartending job too. He worked at the one saloon that had rarely been complained about, not so much a saloon as a kind of club, a place where sandwiches as well as liquor were available to order and where the officers of the post had been accustomed to gather when they came to town.

On this particular morning the bartender had much on his mind. He was brooding over his family troubles—or so he said later. He was worrying about losing his job—which certainly could have been true. Business had all but died with the departure of the troops a few days before. These morning hours were dull. They passed on towards midday and the only customers there were two beer drinkers playing cards at a rear table. And an old Indian wrapped in a dirty old buffalo robe despite the warmth of the weather came in at the door and sat down at one of the front tables near the bar.

The bartender knew this Indian, knew him by frequent sight and serving at least. It was unusual for an Indian to be in that saloon, but this Indian had been there often during the previous months, always with a group of middle-aged officers, had sat at that same table in that same chair, not exactly a part of the group yet with it, sitting silent there with the officers and drinking when they drank and sometimes nodding his head gravely at what was said. Now he was alone. The officers were hundreds of miles away, riding towards the port from which they would embark for Cuba.

The old Indian sat stiff and still on the chair and the bartender

8

watched him and a familiar anger began to burn in the bartender's mind.

That was one thing the bartender hated, serving drinks to a dirty Indian. What right did one of these smelly thieving old men with his dirty coppery skin and ugly face have to come into a white man's place and drink a white man's liquor and expect a white man to serve it to him? The way to handle Indians was to throw them the stuff by the bottle, sell them the cheapest and make them pay plenty and go drink themselves silly outside in some gutter.

The old Indian moved on the chair. He raised a hand to catch the bartender's attention as the officers had always done. 'Whisky,' he said as the officers had always said. 'The best.'

For a moment the bartender thought of jumping over the bar and grabbing hold of the Indian and throwing him bodily out into the road. No. His employer was somewhere in the back room and would hear the noise and his employer was in no mood to accept the loss of a customer, any customer. The bartender took a whisky glass and reached under the bar to the jar on the shelf there in which the dregs left in used glasses were poured. It had not been emptied for several days. He dipped the whisky glass in and brought it out dripping with the dirty mixture. He walked around the end of the bar and to the table and set the glass on it. Fifty cents was the top price for a single drink. No one was ever expected to settle his bill until ready to leave. But the bartender stood there looking down at the Indian. 'One dollar,' he said. 'Now.'

The Indian looked up at him. Slowly he put one hand inside the discoloured old buffalo robe. He took a long time finding what he sought. A slow satisfaction began to build in the bartender and then suddenly faded as the Indian laid a silver dollar on the table. The bartender reached for it and the anger burning once more in his mind made his hand shake and he dropped the coin and it fell to the floor and rolled. He bent to pick it up and as he did so he heard a chuckle from back by the rear table and the sound increased the fire in his mind. He grabbed the coin and went again behind the bar and leaned against it staring at the old Indian and the whisky glass filled with the jar's dregs.

9

The old Indian lifted the glass in his right hand. He looked around the empty table and raised the glass a little higher as if in greeting. He put the glass to his lips and took a first swallow into his mouth and his head dropped forward and he spat the stuff out and then was still, sitting quiet in the chair, staring at the glass in his hand. He sat there motionless for perhaps a full moment. He rose, still holding the glass, and went straight to the bar and set the glass down and looked over it at the bartender. 'Not good,' he said.

Those were the last words the old Indian ever spoke, for the anger in the bartender flamed upward and destroyed all restraint and he reached and took the revolver that lay on the shelf beneath the bar and brought it up for the purpose, he said later, of forcing the complaining old fool to drink the stuff anyway, but the Indian read more than that in his eyes and knew and dropped below the bar level, clutching his old robe about him to escape and the bartender leaned and reached over and fired. The bullet drove downward through the Indian's neck into his body. He slipped to the floor and rolled over and was still. He was dead before the two beer drinkers at the rear table had risen to their feet to come running forward.

There had to be a trial so there was a trial. A man had been killed and in the presence of two witnesses. But no one was very enthusiastic about it. The prosecution was not a strong one and simply did what by law it had to do. The old Indian was as alone in death as he had been those last moments in the saloon. His officer friends were far away, travelling towards a new military frontier. Even those of his own race quickly, and perhaps wisely, disappeared from the neighbourhood of the town when they heard what had happened.

It was a peculiar trial in one respect. The original charge was murder. That was changed to manslaughter, then raised to murder again—at the request, no less, of the bartender's lawyer himself. But that lawyer knew what he was doing. He was aiming at a direct acquittal. He pleaded self-defence for his client. He pushed aside the fact that the old Indian was unarmed. How could his client have been certain that the old fool didn't have a gun or a knife concealed under that buffalo robe and wasn't bending down to pull it and then come after him? The jurymen took that chance immediately. They were out less than ten minutes. Not guilty. 'There was nothing to get excited about,' one of them said later. 'It was just an Indian. What's another one of them more or less?'

Just another Indian. The almost casual opening testimony establishing some identity for this Indian offered a few facts bearing on that point. When he was younger he had served as an Army guide. He walked with a stiffness in his right leg and two fingers of his left hand were missing.

Third, an article in a small local weekly newspaper published in a Montana mining camp in 1901. The jump this time is three years and more than half a thousand miles. But again the mind can make it if the will helps.

The man who wrote the article, probably the editor of the local weekly, because the paper could scarcely have supported more than a one-man staff, really did his best in the writing. He filled nearly two columns of the single-sheet issue with it, wordy, boastful, strongly personal in the tradition of western journalism of the period, well filled with official phrases about the qualities of the enterprising settlement in glorious Montana in which he was privileged to live and hold a position of civic responsibility in the opening years of the bright new century called the twentieth. He was variously shocked, disgusted, startled, outraged at what had happened. He was thunderingly insistent that something should be done about it but not quite certain what. It is possible that he wrote to some extent with his tongue in his cheek. That highly successful camp in Montana, even in 1901, was not exactly a quiet community.

A man had been killed.

Everyone knew him, so the writer said. Everyone knew everyone else in that settlement so new that the census of the year before had passed it by. He was the man who looked after the bar in the larger of the camp's two saloons where you could get every kind of liquid refreshment. Was there ever a citizen of the camp who had not gone into that saloon tired and thirsty from getting gold or copper out of the hard unyielding rock and been grateful to see that red-headed talkative man waiting behind the bar to serve that liquid refreshment? What if the name he used was likely not the name his parents had given him? He served good drinks. What if he had come up to Montana from down Kansas way with a some-what vague reputation of being a dangerous man in anger? He served good drinks and served them well. He was free, white, and well past twenty-one, with the usual supposedly complete right to life, liberty, and the pursuit of happiness.[1] And he was dead. Ah, the changes of fate.

So much for the journal. What had happened was in itself short and simple. And deadly serious. This man, this bartender, had opened the place as usual about ten o'clock in the morning. Most of the men of the camp were out at the diggings and had been for hours.

He was behind the bar, wiping glasses and arranging them on a shelf. One customer was there, almost hidden in a corner, a miner whose claim had proved to be nothing and who was already start-ing the new day's drowning of his misfortune. And a man wearing an old hat and a shapeless old overcoat came in and went straight to the bar and spoke to the bartender in a low voice. The bartender turned quickly from the shelf and stared at the man and dropped the glass he was holding and the man took a revolver from the right-hand pocket of the old overcoat and fired and shot the bar-tender neatly through the heart. The man turned and saw the miner in the corner half out of his chair and staring. 'Don't be in a hurry to follow me,' the man said. The miner wasn't. The man went out of the door and around the side of the building and was gone. The only trace of him found afterwards was a neatly rolled bundle under a bush a half-mile away, the revolver and the hat pushed inside the rolled overcoat. They offered no identification. Hoofprints of a horse were found nearby, but the trail faded out in the rocky country.

[1] Life, liberty, and the pursuit of happiness: Quotation from the American Declaration of Independence, 1776. Also note that at the age of twenty-one a man or woman is supposed to be a fully responsible person.

There is only one more important point. That miner was the only eye-witness. The killing had happened so quickly and the man's hat had shadowed his face so completely that the miner had difficulty trying to describe him. It seemed to him, the miner said, that the man walked and stood very erect like someone who had seen a lot of military service. And he thought, he wasn't certain, but he thought the man had a scar along the side of his jaw.

Of course that man had a scar. He had to have it. A scar made by a stone in a gully in New Mexico sixteen years before.

Mr Higginbotham's Catastrophe

NATHANIEL HAWTHORNE

Nathaniel Hawthorne (1804–1864) is a strange and original American genius, whose novels are full of stern sense and exact and beautiful use of words. Much of his working life was spent as an official representative of the United States government, and this gave him the security he needed to be able to work at his books in peace. He was a slow worker and his production is small. His finest novels are *The Scarlet Letter* and *The House of the Seven Gables*; he also wrote about some of the Greek stories in *The Tanglewood Tales*. The following short story shows Hawthorne in a lighter fashion.

A YOUNG fellow, a tobacco pedlar by trade, was on his way from Morristown, where he had dealt largely with the Deacon of the Shaker[1] settlement, to the village of Parker's Falls, on Salmon River. He had a neat little cart, painted green, with a box of cigars shown on each side, and an Indian chief, holding a pipe and a golden tobacco stalk, on the rear. The pedlar drove a smart little horse, and was a young man of excellent character, keen at a bargain, but none the worse liked by the Yankees; who, as I have heard them say, would rather be shaved with a sharp razor than a dull one. Especially was he admired by the pretty girls along the Connecticut, whose favour he used to obtain by presents of the best smoking tobacco in his stock; knowing well that the country girls of New England are generally great performers on pipes.

[1] Shaker: a religious group.

Moreover, as will be seen in the course of my story, the pedlar was curious, and something of a talker, always wanting to hear the news and anxious to tell it again.

After an early breakfast at Morristown, the tobacco pedlar whose name was Dominicus Pike, had travelled seven mile through a lonely piece of woods, without speaking a word to any body but himself and his little grey horse. It being nearly seven o'clock, he was as eager to hold a morning gossip as a city shop keeper to read the morning paper. An opportunity seemed at hand when, after lighting a cigar with a sun-glass, he looked up, and saw a man coming over the brow of the hill, at the foot of which the pedlar had stopped his green cart. Dominicus watched him as he walked down, and noticed that he carried a bundle over his shoulder on the end of a stick, and travelled with a weary, yet determined pace. He did not look as if he had started in the freshness of the morning, but had travelled all night, and meant to do the same all day.

'Good morning, mister,' said Dominicus, when within speaking distance. 'You go a pretty good speed. What's the latest news at Parker's Falls?'

The man pulled the broad edge of a grey hat over his eyes and answered, rather sullenly, that he did not come from Parker's Falls, which, as being the extent of his own day's journey, the pedlar had naturally mentioned in his enquiry.

'Well, then,' replied Dominicus Pike, 'let's have the latest news where you did come from. I'm not particular about Parker's Falls. Any place will do.'

Being thus encouraged, the traveller—who was as ill-looking a fellow as one would desire to meet in a lonely piece of woods— appeared to hesitate a little, as if he was either searching his memory for news, or weighing the usefulness of telling it. At last, climbing on the step of the cart, he whispered in the ear of Dominicus, though he might have shouted aloud and no other mortal would have heard him.

'I do remember one little trifle of news,' said he. 'Old Mr Higginbotham, of Kimballton, was murdered in his orchard at

ight o'clock last night, by an Irishman and a nigger. They hung
im up to the branch of a St Michael's pear-tree, where nobody
vould find him till the morning.'

As soon as this horrible news was told, the stranger took himself
o his journey again, with more speed than ever, not even turning
is head when Dominicus invited him to smoke a Spanish cigar
.nd tell him all the details. The pedlar whistled to his horse and
vent up the hill, thinking about the unhappy fate of Mr Higgin-
ɔotham whom he had known in the way of trade, having sold him
nany and various types of tobacco. He was rather astonished at
he speed with which the news had spread. Kimballton was nearly
sixty miles distant in a straight line; the murder had been committed only at eight o'clock the previous night; yet Dominicus had
heard of it at seven in the morning, when, in all probability, poor
Mr Higginbotham's own family had only just discovered his
corpse, hanging on the St Michael's pear-tree. The stranger
on foot must be a quite remarkable walker to travel at such a
rate.

'Ill news flies fast, they say,' thought Dominicus Pike; 'but this
beats railroads. The fellow ought to be hired to go express with
the President's Message.'

The difficulty was solved by supposing that the speaker had
made a mistake of one day in the date of the event; so that our
friend did not hesitate to introduce the story at every inn and
country store along the road. He always found himself the first
bearer of the news, and was so bothered with questions that he
could not avoid filling up the outline, till it became quite a respectable narrative. He met with one piece of evidence that helped to
prove his tale. Mr Higginbotham was a trader; and a former clerk
of his, to whom Dominicus told the facts, testified that the old
gentleman was accustomed to return home through the orchard
about nightfall, with the money and valuable papers of the store in
his pocket. The clerk showed little grief at Mr Higginbotham's
catastrophe, hinting, what the pedlar had discovered in his own
dealings with him, that he was an awkward old fellow, as mean as a

17

vice. His property would descend to a pretty niece who was now
keeping school in Kimballton.

What with telling the news for the public good, and driving
bargains for his own, Dominicus was so much delayed on the road
that he chose to put up at an inn, about five miles from Parker's
Falls. After supper, lighting one of his best cigars, he seated himself in the bar-room, and went through the story of the murder
which had grown so fast that it took him half an hour to tell. There
were as many as twenty people in the room, nineteen of whom
received it all for gospel. But the twentieth was an elderly farmer
who had arrived on horseback a short time before, and was now
seated in a corner smoking his pipe.

When the story was concluded, he rose up very slowly, brought
his chair right in front of Dominicus, and stared him full in the
face, puffing out the worst tobacco smoke the pedlar had ever smelt.

'Will you take an oath,' demanded he, in the tone of a country
justice at an examination, 'that old Squire Higginbotham of Kimballton was murdered in his orchard the night before last, and
found hanging on his great pear-tree yesterday morning?'

'I tell the story as I heard it, mister,' answered Dominicus,
dropping his half-burnt cigar; 'I don't say that I saw the thing
done. So I can't take my oath that he was murdered exactly in that
way.'

'But I can take mine,' said the farmer, 'that if Squire Higginbotham was murdered night before last, I drank a glass with his
ghost this morning. Being a neighbour of mine, he called me into
his store, as I was riding by, and treated me, and then asked me to
do a little business for him on the road. He didn't seem to know
any more about his own murder than I did.'

'Why, then, it can't be a fact!' exclaimed Dominicus Pike.

'I guess he'd have mentioned it, if it was,' said the old farmer;
and he removed his chair back to the corner, leaving Dominicus
unhappy indeed.

Here was a sad resurrection of old Mr Higginbotham! The
pedlar had no heart to mix in the conversation any more, but

comforted himself with a glass of gin and water, and went to bed where, all night long, he dreamed of hanging on the St Michael's pear-tree. To avoid the old farmer (whom he so disliked that his hanging would have pleased him better than Mr Higginbotham's), Dominicus rose in the grey of the morning, put the little horse into the green cart, and trotted swiftly away to Parker's Falls. The fresh breeze, the dewy road, and the pleasant summer dawn, increased his spirits, and might have encouraged him to repeat the old story had there been anybody awake to hear it. But he met neither ox team, light wagon, horseman, nor foot traveller, till, just as he crossed the Salmon River, a man came trudging down to the bridge with a bundle over his shoulder, on the end of a stick.

'Good morning, mister,' said the pedlar, slowing down his horse. 'If you come from Kimballton or that neighbourhood, maybe you can tell me the real fact about this affair of old Mr Higginbotham. Was the old fellow actually murdered two or three nights ago, by an Irishman and a nigger?'

Dominicus had spoken in too great a hurry to observe, at first, that the stranger himself had quite a touch of negro blood. On hearing this sudden question, the Ethiopian appeared to change his skin, its yellow colour becoming a terrible white, while, shaking and stammering, he thus replied:

'No! No! There was no coloured man! It was an Irishman that hanged him last night, at eight o'clock. I came away at seven! His folks can't have looked for him yet in the orchard.'

Scarcely had the man spoken, when he interrupted himself and, though he seemed weary enough before, continued his journey at a pace which would have kept the pedlar's horse at a quick trot. Dominicus stared after him in great wonder. If the murder had not been committed till Tuesday night, who was the prophet that had foretold it, in all its circumstances, on Tuesday morning? If Mr Higginbotham's corpse were not yet discovered by his own family, how came this man, at over thirty miles distance, to know that he was hanging in the orchard, especially as he had left Kimballton before the unfortunate man was hanged at all? These

peculiar circumstances, with the stranger's surprise and terro
made Dominicus think of raising a hue and cry after him, as a
accomplice in the murder; since a murder, it seemed, had real'
been committed.

With these thoughts, Dominicus Pike drove into the street o
Parker's Falls, which, as everybody knows, is as prosperous
village as three cotton factories and a mill can make it. Th
machinery was not in motion, and only a few of the shop doo
unbarred, when he got off in the stable yard of the inn, and mad
it his first business to order the horse four quarts of oats. H
second duty, of course, was to tell of Mr Higginbotham's cata
trophe to the inn-keeper. He thought it advisable, however, not t
be too definite as to the date of the dreadful fact, and also to b
uncertain whether it was committed by an Irishman and a negro
or by the Irishman alone. Neither did he try to tell it on his ow
authority, or that of any one person; but mentioned it as a repo
generally spread about.

The story ran through the town like fire among dry trees, an
became so much the universal talk that nobody could tell whenc
it had started. Mr Higginbotham was as well known at Parker'
Falls as any citizen of the place, being part owner of the mill, and
considerable stockholder in the cotton factories. The inhabitant
felt their own prosperity was concerned in his fate. Such was th
excitement, that the Parker's Falls *Gazette* anticipated it
regular day of publication, and came out with a column emphasize
with capitals, and headed HORRID MURDER OF MR HIGGINBOTHAM
Among other dreadful details, the printed account described th
mark of the cord round the dead man's neck, and stated the num
ber of thousand dollars of which he had been robbed; there wa
much pathos also about the state of his niece, who had gone from
one fainting fit to another, ever since her uncle was found hanging
on the St Michael's pear-tree with his pockets inside out. The
village poet also commemorated the young lady's grief in seven
teen verses of a ballad. The town council held a meeting, and, in
consideration of Mr Higginbotham's claims on the town, deter
mined to issue handbills offering a reward of five hundred dollar

or the taking of his murderers, and the recovery of the stolen property.

Meanwhile the whole population of Parker's Falls, consisting of shopkeepers, mistresses of boarding-houses, factory girls, mill men, and schoolboys, rushed into the street and kept up such a terrible talking as more than made up for the silence of the cotton machines, which refrained from their usual noise out of respect for the dead. Had Mr Higginbotham cared about fame after death, his ghost would have rejoiced in this. Our friend Dominicus, in his vanity of heart, forgot his intended precautions, and getting up in the middle of the town, announced himself as the bearer of the true information which had caused so wonderful a sensation. He immediately became the great man of the moment, and had just begun a new edition of the story, with a voice like a preacher, when the mail coach drove into the village street. It had travelled all night, and must have changed horses at Kimballton, at three in the morning.

The coach went up to the yard of the inn, followed by a thousand people; for if any man had been minding his own business till then, he now left it at sixes and sevens, to hear the news. The pedlar, first in the race, discovered two passengers, both of whom had been startled from a comfortable sleep to find themselves in the centre of a noisy crowd. Every man attacking them with separate questions, all asked at once, the couple were struck speechless, though one was a lawyer and the other a young lady.

'Mr Higginbotham! Mr Higginbotham! Tell us the particulars about old Mr Higginbotham!' shouted the crowd. 'What is the coroner's verdict? Are the murderers taken? Is Mr Higginbotham's niece come out of her fainting fits? Mr Higginbotham! Mr Higginbotham!'

The coachman said not a word, except to swear awfully at the inn-keeper for not bringing him a fresh team of horses. The lawyer inside had generally his wits about him even when asleep; the first thing he did, after learning the cause of the excitement, was to produce a large, red pocket-book. Meantime Dominicus Pike,

being an extremely polite young man, and also suspecting that
female tongue would tell the story as well as a lawyer's, ha
handed the lady out of the coach. She was a fine, smart girl, no
wide awake and bright as a button, and had such a sweet, prett
mouth, that Dominicus would rather have heard a love tale fro:
it than a tale of murder.

'Gentlemen and ladies,' said the lawyer to the shop-keepers, th
mill men, and the factory girls, 'I can assure you that some drea
ful mistake, or, more probably, a deliberate falsehood, wicked
made to injure Mr Higginbotham's reputation, has caused th
remarkable uproar. We passed through Kimballton at thro
o'clock this morning, and most certainly should have been ir
formed of the murder had any been committed. But I have proc
nearly as strong as Mr Higginbotham's own oral testimony, in th
negative. Here is a note concerning a case of his in the Connecti
courts, which was delivered me from that gentleman himself.
find it dated at ten o'clock last evening.'

So saying, the lawyer showed the date and signature of the not
which most completely proved, either that this difficult M
Higginbotham was alive when he wrote it, or—as some thoug
the more probable case of two doubtful ones—that he was s
absorbed in worldly business as to continue to do it even after h
death. But unexpected evidence was forthcoming. The young lad
after listening to the pedlar's explanation, merely seized a momen
to smooth her gown and put her curls in order, and then appeare
at the inn door, making a modest signal to be heard.

'Good people,' said she, 'I am Mr Higginbotham's niece.'

A wondering murmur passed through the crowd on beholdin
her so rosy and bright; that same unhappy niece, whom they ha
supposed, on the authority of the Parker's Falls *Gazette*, to b
lying at death's door in a fainting fit. But some shrewd fellows ha
doubted, all along, whether a young lady would be quite so des
perate at the hanging of a rich old uncle.

'You see,' continued Miss Higginbotham, with a smile, 'tha
this strange story is quite unfounded as to myself; and I believe
may declare it to be equally so in regard to my dear Uncle Higgin

22

otham. He has the kindness to give me a home in his house, though I contribute to my own support by teaching a school. I left Kimballton this morning to spend a vacation with a friend, about five miles from Parker's Falls. My generous uncle, when he heard me on the stairs, called me to his bedside, and gave me two dollars and fifty cents to pay my fare, and another dollar for my extra expenses. He then laid his pocket-book under his pillow, shook hands with me, and advised me to take some biscuit in my bag, instead of breakfasting on the road. I feel confident, therefore, that I left my beloved relative alive, and trust that I shall find him so when I return.'

The young lady bowed at the close of her speech, which was so sensible and well worded, and delivered with such grace and propriety, that everybody thought her fit to be teacher of the best academy in the State. But a stranger would have supposed that Mr Higginbotham was an object of hatred at Parker's Falls, and that a thanksgiving had been proclaimed for his murder; so great was the anger of the inhabitants on learning their mistake. The mill men decided to give public honours to Dominicus Pike, only hesitating whether to tar and feather[1] him, or refresh him at the town pump, on the top of which he had declared himself the bearer of the news. The town council, by advice of the lawyer, spoke of prosecuting him for circulating unfounded reports, to the great disturbance of the peace of the Commonwealth. Nothing saved Dominicus, either from mob law or a court of justice, but an eloquent appeal made by the young lady in his behalf. Addressing a few words of heartfelt gratitude to the young lady, he climbed the green cart and rode out of town, fired at by the schoolboys with sticks and lumps of clay. As he turned his head for a farewell glance with Mr Higginbotham's niece, a ball of mud hit him right in the mouth, giving him a most grim appearance. His whole person was so covered with mud that he had almost a mind to ride back, and ask for the threatened wash at the town pump; for, though not meant in kindness, it would now have been a deed of charity.

However, the sun shone bright on poor Dominicus, and the

[1] Tar and feather: punish someone by covering with tar and feathers.

mud was easily brushed off when dry. Being a funny chap, hi
heart soon cheered up; nor could he stop from laughing heartil
at the uproar which his story had caused. The handbills of th
town would cause the imprisonment of all the vagabonds in th
State; the paragraph in the Parker's Falls *Gazette* would be re
printed from Maine to Florida, and perhaps form an item in th
London newspapers; and many a miser would tremble for hi
money bags and life, on learning the catastrophe of Mr Higgin
botham. The pedlar thought much of the charms of the youn
schoolmistress, and swore that Daniel Webster[1] never spoke no
looked so like an angel as Miss Higginbotham, while defendin
him from the angry people at Parker's Falls.

Dominicus was now on the Kimballton road, having all alon
decided to visit that place though business had drawn him out o
the most direct road from Morristown. As he approached th
scene of the supposed murder, he continued to turn the circum
stances in his mind, and was astonished at the look that the whol
case had. If nothing had occurred to confirm the story of the firs
traveller, it might now be considered as a joke; but the yellow ma
was evidently acquainted either with the report or the fact; an
there was a mystery in his uneasy and guilty look on being abruptl
questioned. When, to this unusual combination of incidents, it wa
added that the rumour agreed exactly with Mr Higginbotham's
character and habits of life, and that he had an orchard, and a St
Michael's pear-tree, near which he always passed at nightfall: th
surrounding evidence appeared so strong that Dominicus doubted
whether the autograph produced by the lawyer, or even the niece's
direct testimony, ought to be equal to it. Making cautious en
quiries along the road, the pedlar further learned that Mr Higgin
botham had in his service an Irishman of doubtful character, whom
he had hired without a recommendation, because of economy.

'May I be hanged myself,' exclaimed Dominicus Pike aloud, on
reaching the top of a lonely hill, 'if I'll believe old Higginbotham
is unhanged till I see him with my own eyes, and hear it from his

[1] Daniel Webster, 1782–1852, famous for his appearance and his fine
speaking.

wn mouth! And as he's a really funny chap, I'll have the minister or some other responsible man to help me prove it.'

It was growing dark when he reached the toll-house on Kimballton road, about a quarter of a mile from the village of this name. His little cart was fast bringing him up with a man on horseback, who trotted through the gate a short distance in front of him, nodded to the toll-gatherer, and kept on towards the village. Dominicus was acquainted with the tollman, and while making change, the usual remarks on the weather passed between them.

'I suppose,' said the pedlar, 'you have not seen anything of old Mr Higginbotham within a day or two?'

'Yes,' answered the toll-gatherer. 'He passed the gate just before you drove up, and there he rides now, if you can see him through the dark. He's been to Woodfield this afternoon, attending a sale there. The old man generally shakes hands and has a little chat with me; but tonight, he nodded—as if to say, "Charge my toll"—and went on; for wherever he goes, he must always be at home by eight o'clock.'

'So they tell me,' said Dominicus.

'I never saw a man look so yellow and thin as the squire does,' continued the toll-gatherer. 'Says I to myself, tonight, he's more like a ghost or an old mummy than good flesh and blood.'

The pedlar strained his eyes through the dark, and could just see the horseman now far ahead on the village road. He seemed to recognize the rear of Mr Higginbotham; but through the evening shadows, and amid the dust from the horse's feet, the figure appeared dim and unsubstantial; as if the shape of the mysterious old man were faintly made of darkness and grey light. Dominicus shivered.

'Mr Higginbotham has come back from the other world, by way of the Kimballton road,' thought he.

He shook the reins and rode forward, keeping about the same distance in the rear of the grey old shadow, till the latter was hidden by a bend of the road. On reaching this point, the pedlar no longer saw the man on horseback, but found himself at the head of the village street, not far from a number of stores and two inns,

25

around the meeting-house tower. On his left were a stone wall an
a gate, the boundary of a wood-yard, beyond which lay an orchar
farther still, a mowing field, and last of all, a house. These wei
the property of Mr Higginbotham, whose dwelling stood besic
the old highway, but had been left in the background by the Kin
ballton toll-gate. Dominicus knew the place; and the little hors
stopped short by instinct; for he was not conscious of tightenir
the reins.

'For the soul of me, I cannot get by this gate!' said he, trem
bling. 'I never shall be my own man again, till I see whether N
Higginbotham is hanging on the St Michael's pear-tree!'

He leaped from the cart, gave the rein a turn round the gar
post, and ran along the green path of the wood-yard as if Old Nick
were chasing behind. Just then the village clock tolled eight, an
as each deep stroke fell, Dominicus gave a fresh jump and fle
faster than before, till, dim in the lonely centre of the orchard, h
saw the fated pear-tree. One great branch stretched from the ob
twisted trunk across the path, and threw the darkest shadow o
that one spot. But something seemed to struggle beneath th
branch.

The pedlar had never pretended to more courage than suits
man of peaceful occupation, nor could he explain his feelings i
this awful emergency. Certain it is, however, that he rushed for
ward, knocked down a strong Irishman with the end of his whip
and found—not indeed hanging on the St Michael's pear-tree
but trembling beneath it, with a rope round his neck—the old
identical Mr Higginbotham!

'Mr Higginbotham,' said Dominicus fearfully, 'you're a
honest man, and I'll take your word for it. Have you been hange
or not?'

If the riddle be not already guessed, a few words will explain th
simple machinery by which this 'coming event' was made to 'cas
its shadow before'. Three men had plotted the robbery and murde
of Mr Higginbotham; two of them, in turn, lost courage and fled
each delaying the crime one night by their disappearance; th

¹ Old Nick: the Devil.

hird was in the act of committing it, when a champion, blindly obeying the call of fate, like the heroes of old romance, appeared in the person of Dominicus Pike.

It only remains to say that Mr Higginbotham took the pedlar into high favour, was pleased to see him marry the pretty school-mistress, and settled his whole property on their children, giving themselves the interest. In due time, the old gentleman, as the climax of his favours, died a Christian death, in bed, since which melancholy event Dominicus Pike has removed from Kimballton, and established a large tobacco factory in my native village.

The Ransom of Red Chief

O. HENRY

O. Henry (1862–1910) had an unsettled life that included
five years in prison—where he began his career as a short-
story writer. In all he wrote six hundred, some of them
being collected in book form under titles such as *Cabbages
and Kings*, and *The Four Million*. As many of the stories
were written for newspapers, he had to keep them short
and give them the kind of surprise ending that would
appeal to quick readers. His style has often been imitated
but at its best remains his own and unique.

I T looked like a good thing: but wait till I tell you. We were down
South, in Alabama—Bill Driscoll and myself—when this kidnapping idea struck us. It was, as Bill afterwards expressed it,
'during a moment of temporary mental apparition'[1] but we didn't
find that out till later.

There was a town down there, as flat as a cake, and called Summit, of course. It contained inhabitants of as self-satisfied a class of
peasants as ever you could imagine.

Bill and me had a joint capital of about six hundred dollars, and
we needed just two thousand dollars to be able to accomplish an
illegal land-buying plan in Western Illinois. We talked it over on
the front steps of the hotel. Love of children, says we, is strong in
country communities; therefore, and for other reasons, a kidnapping plan ought to do better there than near to those newspapers that send reporters out in plain clothes to stir up talk about
such things. We knew that Summit couldn't get after us with

[1] Apparition: wrongly used for 'aberration' or mistake caused by
wandering attention.

nything stronger than constables and, maybe, some lazy dogs and
n article or two in the Weekly Farmers' newspaper. So, it looked
ood.

We selected for our victim the only child of an important citizen
amed Ebenezer Dorset. The father was respectable and mean, a
nan in the building trade and a stern, upright man. The kid was a
oy of ten, with freckles, and hair the colour of the cover of the
nagazine you buy at the news-stand when you want to catch a
rain. Bill and me thought that Ebenezer would offer a ransom of
t least two thousand dollars. But wait till I tell you.

About two miles from Summit was a little mountain, covered
vith a dense wood. On the rear of this mountain was a cave. There
ve stored food.

One evening after sundown, we drove in a cart past old Dorset's
nouse. The kid was in the street, throwing rocks at a kitten on the
pposite fence.

'Hey, little boy!' says Bill, 'would you like to have a bag of
andy and a nice ride?'

The boy catches Bill neatly in the eye with a piece of brick.

'That will cost the old man an extra five hundred dollars,' says
Bill, climbing down.

That boy put up a fight like a middle-sized bear; but, at last, we
got him down in the bottom of the cart and drove away. We took
him up to the cave, and I tied the horse up in the wood. After dark
drove the cart to the little village, three miles away, where we
nad hired it, and walked back to the mountain.

Bill was putting plaster over the scratches and bruises on his
ace. There was a fire burning behind the big rock at the entrance
of the cave, and the boy was watching a pot of boiling coffee, with
wo tail-feathers stuck in his red hair. He points a stick at me when
I come up, and says:

'Ha! cursed paleface, do you dare to enter the camp of Red
Chief, the terror of the plains?'

'He's all right now,' says Bill, rolling up his trousers and
examining some bruises on his legs. 'We're playing Indians, and
we'll give the kid the show of his lifetime.'

Yes, sir, that boy seemed to be having the time of his life. The fun of camping out in a cave had made him forget that he was a prisoner himself. He immediately christened me Snake-eye, the Spy, and announced that, when his braves returned from the war path, I was to be boiled at the stake at the rising of the sun.

Then we had supper: and he filled his mouth full of bacon and gravy, and began to talk. He made a during-dinner speech something like this:

'I like this fine. I never camped out before; but I had a pet wild-cat once, and I was nine last birthday. I hate to go to school. Rats ate up sixteen of Jimmy Talbot's aunt's hen's eggs. Are there any real Indians in this wood? I want some more gravy. Does the trees moving make the wind blow? We had five puppies. What makes your nose so red, Hank? My father has lots of money. Are the stars hot? I beat Ed Walker twice, Saturday. I don't like girls. You can't catch toads unless with a string. Do oxen make any noise? Why are oranges round? Have you got beds to sleep on in this cave? Amos Murray has got six toes. A parrot can talk, but a monkey or a fish can't. How many does it take to make twelve?'

Every few minutes he would remember that he was an Indian and pick up his stick rifle and go softly to the mouth of the cave to search for the spies of the hated paleface. Now and then he would let out a war-cry that was a terror to Old Hank. That boy had Bill frightened from the start.

'Red Chief,' says I to the kid, 'would you like to go home?'

'Aw, what for?' says he. 'I don't have any fun at home. I hate to go to school. I like to camp out. You won't take me back home again, Snake-eye, will you?'

'Not right away,' says I. 'We'll stay in the cave a while.'

'All right!' says he. 'That'll be fine. I never had such fun in all my life.'

We went to bed about eleven o'clock. We spread down some wide, thick blankets and put Red Chief between us. We weren't afraid he'd run away. He kept us awake for three hours, jumping up and reaching for his rifle and crying out, 'Listen, friend,' in mine and Bill's ears, as the fancied crackle of a twig or the rustle of a eaf revealed to his young imagination the secret approach of the outlaws. At last I fell into a troubled sleep, and dreamed that I had been kidnapped and chained to a tree by a fierce pirate with red hair.

Just at daybreak, I was awakened by a series of awful screams from Bill. They weren't howls or shouts such as you'd expect from a manly set of vocal organs—they were simply indecent, terrifying, humiliating screams, such as women give out when they see ghosts or caterpillars. It's an awful thing to hear a strong, desperate, fat man scream suddenly in a cave at daybreak.

I jumped up to see what the matter was. Red Chief was sitting on Bill's chest, with one hand twisted in Bill's hair. In the other he had the sharp knife we used for slicing bacon; and he was very carefully trying to take Bill's scalp, according to the sentence that had been laid upon him the evening before.

I got the knife away from the kid, and made him lie down again. But, from that moment, Bill's spirit was broken. He laid down on his side of the bed, but he never closed an eye again in sleep as long as that boy was with us. I went to sleep for a while, but along towards sun-up I remembered that Red Chief had said I was to be burned at the stake at the rising of the sun. I wasn't nervous or afraid; but I sat up and lit my pipe and leaned against a rock.

'What are you getting up so soon for, Sam?' asked Bill.

'Me?' says I. 'Oh, I got a kind of pain in my shoulder. I thought sitting up would rest it.'

'You're a liar!' says Bill. 'You're afraid. You was to be burned at sunrise, and you was afraid he'd do it. And he would too, if he could find a match. Ain't it awful, Sam? Do you think anybody will pay out money to get a little wretch like that back home?'

'Sure,' said I. 'A noisy kid like that is just the kind that parents love. Now, you and the Chief get up and cook breakfast, while I go up on the top of this mountain and have a look round.'

I went up to the top of the little mountain and ran my eye over the surrounding country. Over towards Summit I expected to see the strong peasants of the village armed with farm tools beating the countryside for the kidnappers. But what I saw was a peaceful landscape dotted with one man ploughing with a horse. Nobody was searching the river; no messengers dashed here and there bringing no news to the worried parents. There was a feeling of sleepiness over the whole outward surface of Alabama that lay open to my view. 'Perhaps,' says I to myself, 'it has not yet been discovered that the wolves have carried away the tender lamb from the fold. Heaven help the wolves!' says I, and I went down the mountain to breakfast.

When I got to the cave I found Bill up against the side of it breathing hard, and the boy threatening to smash him with a rock half as big as a coconut.

'He put a red-hot boiled potato down my back,' explained Bill 'and then stood on it with his foot; and I boxed his ears. Have you got a gun on you, Sam?'

I took the rock away from the boy and kind of stopped the argument. 'I'll finish you,' says the kid to Bill. 'No man ever yet struck the Red Chief but what he got paid for it. You better watch out.'

After breakfast the kid takes a piece of leather with strings wrapped around it out of his pocket and goes outside the cave unwinding it.

'What's he up to now?' says Bill, anxiously. 'You don't think he'll run away, do you, Sam?'

'No fear of it,' says I. 'He don't seem to be much of a home body. But we've got to fix up some plan about the ransom. There don't seem to be much excitement around Summit on account of his disappearance; but maybe they haven't realized yet that he's gone. His folks may think he's spending the night with Aunt Jane or one of the neighbours. Anyhow, he'll be missed today. Tonight we must get a message to his father demanding the two thousand dollars for his return.'

Just then we heard a kind of war-cry, such as David might have given out when he knocked down the champion Goliath.[1] It was a sling that Red Chief had pulled out of his pocket, and he was twisting it round his head.

[1] David and Goliath: a story from the Bible in which the young man David knocked down the huge Goliath by means of a sling.

I jumped, and heard a heavy sound and a kind of sigh from Bill, like a horse gives out when you take his saddle off. A rock the size of an egg had caught Bill just behind his left ear. He loosened himself all over and fell in the fire across the frying-pan of hot water for washing the dishes. I dragged him out and poured cold water on his head for half an hour.

By and by, Bill sits up and feels behind his ear and says, 'Sam, do you know who my favourite Biblical character is?'

'Take it easy,' says I. 'You'll come to your senses presently.'

'King Herod,'[1] says he. 'You won't go away and leave me here alone, will you, Sam?'

I went out and caught that boy and shook him until I couldn't shake him any more.

'If you don't behave,' says I, 'I'll take you straight home. Now, are you going to be good, or not?'

'I was only funning,' says he sullenly. 'I didn't mean to hurt Old Hank. But what did he hit me for? I'll behave, Snake-eye, if you won't send me home, and if you'll let me play the Black Scout today.'

'I don't know the game,' says I. 'That's for you and Mr Bill to decide. He's your playmate for the day. I'm going away for a while, on business. Now, you come in and make friends with him and say you are sorry for hurting him, or home you go, at once.'

I made him and Bill shake hands, and then I took Bill aside and told him I was going to Poplar Cove, a little village three miles from the cave, and find out what I could about how the kidnapping had been regarded in Summit. Also, I thought it best to send a sharp letter to old man Dorset that day, demanding the ransom and dictating how it should be paid.

'You know, Sam,' says Bill, 'I've always stood by you in earthquakes, fire and flood—in card games, police raids, train robberies and cyclones. I never lost my nerve yet till we kidnapped that two-legged skyrocket of a kid. He's got me going. You won't leave me long with him, will you, Sam?'

'I'll be back some time this afternoon,' says I. 'You must keep

[1] King Herod: a king in the Bible who killed children.

33

the boy amused and quiet till I return. And now we'll write th
letter to old Dorset.'

Bill and I got paper and pencil and worked on the letter whil
Red Chief, with a blanket wrapped around him, walked up an
down, guarding the mouth of the cave. Bill begged me tearfully t
make the ransom fifteen hundred dollars instead of two thousand
'I ain't attempting,' says he, 'to forget the moral goodness o
parental affection, but we're dealing with humans, and it ain'
human for anybody to give up two thousand dollars for that forty
pound piece of freckled wildcat. I'm willing to take a chance a
fifteen hundred dollars. You can charge the difference up to me.

So, to relieve Bill, I agreed, and together we wrote a letter tha
ran this way:

Ebenezer Dorset, Esq:

We have your boy concealed in a place far from Summit. It i
useless for you or the most skilful detectives to attempt to fin
him. Absolutely the only terms on which you can have him
restored to you are these: we demand fifteen hundred dollars in
large bills for his return; the money to be left at midnight
tonight at the same spot and in the same box as your reply—as
hereinafter described. If you agree to these terms, send your
answer in writing by a single messenger tonight at half-past
eight o'clock. After crossing Owl Creek, on the road to Poplar
Cove, there are three large trees about a hundred yards apart,
close to the fence of the wheat field on the right-hand side. At
the bottom of the fence post, opposite the third tree, will be
found a small pasteboard box.

The messenger will place the answer in this box and return
immediately to Summit.

If you attempt any treachery or fail to agree with our demand
as stated, you will never see your boy again.

If you pay the money as demanded, he will be returned to you
safe and well within three hours. These terms are final, and if
you do not agree to them, no further communication will be
attempted.

Two Desperate Men.

I addressed the letter to Dorset, and put it in my pocket. As I was about to start, the kid comes up to me and says:

'Aw, Snake-eye, you said I could play the Black Scout while you was gone.'

'Play it, of course,' says I. 'Mr Bill will play with you. What kind of a game is it?'

'I'm the Black Scout,' says the Red Chief, 'and I have to ride to the stockade to warn the settlers that the Indians are coming. I'm tired of playing Indian myself. I want to be the Black Scout.'

'All right,' says I. 'It sounds harmless to me. I expect Mr Bill will help you defeat the wild savages.'

'What am I to do?' asks Bill, looking at the kid suspiciously.

'You are the hoss,' says Black Scout. 'Get down on your hands and knees. How can I ride to the stockade without a hoss?'

'You'd better keep him interested,' said I, 'till we get the scheme going. Loosen up.'

Bill gets down on his all fours, and a look comes in his eye like a rabbit's when you catch it in a trap.

'How far is it to the stockade, kid?' he asks, in a strange manner of voice.

'Ninety miles,' says the Black Scout. 'And you have to push yourself to get there on time. Get on, now!'

The Black Scout jumps on Bill's back and digs his heels in his side.

'For heaven's sake,' says Bill, 'hurry back, Sam, as soon as you can. I wish we hadn't made the ransom more than a thousand. Say, you stop kicking me or I'll get up and warm you good.'

I walked over to Poplar Cove and sat around the post office and store, talking with the real old ones that came in to trade. One bearded chap says that he hears Summit is all upset on account of old Ebenezer Dorset's boy having been lost or stolen. That was all I wanted to know. I bought some smoking tobacco, referred to the price of black-eyed peas, posted my letter secretly and came away. The postmaster said the mail-cart would come by in an hour to take the mail on to Summit.

When I got back to the cave Bill and the boy were not to be found. I explored the vicinity of the cave, and risked a shout or two, but there was no reply.

So I lighted my pipe and sat down on a grassy bank to await developments.

In about half an hour I heard the bushes rustle, and Bill rocked out into the little clearing in front of the cave. Behind him was the kid, stepping softly like a scout with a broad grin on his face. Bill stopped, took off his hat and wiped his face with a red handkerchief. The kid stopped about eight feet behind him.

'Sam,' says Bill, 'I suppose you'll think I'm a fool, but I couldn't help it. I'm a grown person with the masculine habits of self-defence, but there is a time when all these systems fail. The boy is gone. I have sent him home. All is off. There was martyrs in old times,' goes on Bill, 'that suffered death rather than give up the particular kind of cunning they enjoyed. None of 'em was ever forced to suffer such supernatural tortures as I have been. I tried to be faithful to our agreement; but there came a limit.'

'What's the trouble, Bill?' I asks him.

'I was rode,' says Bill, 'the ninety miles to the stockade, not missing an inch. Then, when the settler was rescued, I was given oats. Sand ain't a substitute for that. And then, for an hour I had to try and explain to him why there was nothin' in holes, how a road can run both ways and what makes the grass green. I tell you, Sam, a human can only stand so much. I takes him by the neck of his clothes and drags him down the mountain. On the way he kicks my legs black-and-blue from the knees down; and I've got to have two or three bites on my thumb and hand doctored.'

'But he's gone'—continues Bill—'gone home. I showed him the road to Summit and kicked him about eight feet nearer there at one kick. I'm sorry we lose the ransom; but it was either that or Bill Driscoll to the madhouse.'

Bill is blowing away, but there is a look of tremendous peace and growing content on his rose-pink features.

'Bill,' says I, 'there isn't any heart disease in your family, is there?'

37

'No,' says Bill, 'nothing like that except malaria and accidents. Why?'

'Then you might turn round,' says I, 'and have a look behind you.'

Bill turns and sees the boy, and loses his complexion and sits down right on the ground and begins to pick aimlessly at grass and little sticks. For an hour I was afraid for his mind. And then I told him that my scheme was to put the whole job through immediately and that we would get the ransom and be off with it by midnight if old Dorset agreed with our plan. So Bill improved enough to give the kid a weak sort of smile and a promise to play the Russian in a Japanese war with him as soon as he felt a little better.

I had a scheme for collecting that ransom without danger of being caught by any other plots that ought to recommend itself to professional kidnappers. The tree under which the answer was to be left—and the money later on—was close to the road fence with big, bare fields on all sides. If a gang of constables should be watching for anyone to come for the note they could see him a long way off crossing the fields or in the road. But no, sirree! At half-past eight I was up in the tree as well hidden as a tree toad, waiting for the messenger to arrive.

Exactly on time, a half-grown boy rides up the road on a bicycle, finds the pasteboard box at the foot of the fence-post, slips a folded piece of paper into it and pedals away again back towards Summit.

I waited an hour and then concluded the thing was all right. I slid down the tree, got the note, slipped along the fence till I got to the woods, and was back at the cave in another half an hour. I opened the note, got near the lamp and read it to Bill. It was written with a pen in an awkward hand, and the sum and substance of it was this:

Two Desperate Men,

Gentlemen, I received your letter today by post, in regard to the ransom you ask for the return of my son. I think you are a little high in your demands, and I hereby make you a counter-proposal, which I am inclined to believe you will accept. You bring Johnny home and pay me two hundred and fifty dollars in cash, and I agree to take him off your hands. You had better come at night, for the neighbours believe he is lost, and I couldn't be responsible for what they would do to anybody they saw bringing him back.

Very respectfully,
Ebenezer Dorset.

'Great pirates of Penzance!' says I; 'of all the impudent—'

But I glanced at Bill, and hesitated. He had the most appealing look in his eyes I ever saw on the face of a dumb or a talking brute.

'Sam,' says he, 'what's two hundred and fifty dollars, after all? We've got the money. One more night of this kid will send me to bed in Bedlam. Besides being a thorough gentleman, I think Mr Dorset is generous for making us such an offer. You ain't going to let the chance go, are you?'

'Tell you the truth, Bill,' says I, 'this little lamb has somewhat got on my nerves too. We'll take him home, pay the ransom and make our get-away.'

We took him home that night. We got him to go by telling him that his father had bought a silver rifle and special Indian clothes for him, and we were going to hunt bears the next day.

It was just twelve o'clock when we knocked at Ebenezer's front door. Just at the moment when I should have been taking the fifteen hundred dollars from the box under the tree, according to the original idea, Bill was counting out two hundred and fifty dollars into Dorset's hand.

When the kid found out we were going to leave him at home he started up a howl like a horrible wind and fastened himself as tight as a leech to Bill's leg. His father dragged him off gradually, like a plaster.

'How long can you hold him?' asks Bill.

'I'm not as strong as I used to be,' says old Dorset, 'but I think I can promise you ten minutes.'

'Enough,' says Bill. 'In ten minutes I shall cross the Central,

39

Southern and Middle Western States, and be legging it beautifull for the Canadian border.'

And, as dark as it was, and as fat as Bill was, and as good runner as I am, he was a good mile and a half out of Summit befor I could catch up with him.

A Piece of Pie

DAMON RUNYON

Damon Runyon (1880–1946) wrote on every kind of subject and in every sort of way, and many people thought of him as an inspired journalist. But he is best known as a story teller of New York and the less respectable men and women—or 'guys and dolls' as Runyon preferred to call them—who lived there, and still do. The present story is taken from his first collection in book form, *Guys and Dolls*, and the same title was given to a successful musical play and film made from another of the stories. He is one of the most amusing and entertaining writers that America has produced.

In reading the story that follows, one should remember that in the style of writing Runyon is trying to suggest the efforts of one of his 'guys', or 'characters', to write in very formal English. There are no shortened forms; the present tense is used for all action; but the slang creeps in, as when 'I' and Horsey in this story 'make the race meeting' (attend the horse-races), and Horsey 'gets to going very good' (is very successful with his bets).

ON Boylston Street, in the City of Boston, Massachusetts, there is a place where you can get as nice a boiled lobster as anybody ever pushes a lip over, and who is in there one evening enjoying this nice bit of food but a character by the name of Horse Thief and me.

This Horse Thief is called Horsey for short, and he is not called by this name because he ever steals a horse but because it is the agreed public opinion from coast to coast that he may steal one if the opportunity presents.

Personally, I consider Horsey a very fine character, because any time he is holding anything he is willing to share his good fortune with one and all, and at this time in Boston he is holding plenty. It is the time we make the race meeting at Suffolk Down, and Horsey gets to going very good, indeed, and in fact he is now a character of means, and is host for the boiled lobster.

Well, at a table next to us are four or five characters who all seem to be well-dressed, and stout, and red-faced, and prosperous looking, and who all speak with the true Boston accent, which consists of many ah's and very few r's. Characters such as these are familiar to anybody who is ever in Boston very much, and they are bound to be politicians, retired cops, or builders, because Boston is really quite infested with characters of this nature.

I am paying no attention to them, because they are drinking local ale, and talking loud, and long ago I learn that when a Boston character is engaged in aleing himself up, it is a good idea to let him alone, because the best you can get out of him is maybe a blow on the nose. But Horsey is in there listening hard, and very much interested in their conversation, and finally I listen myself just to hear what is attracting his attention, when one of the characters speaks as follows:

'Well,' he says, 'I am willing to bet ten thousand dollars that he can outeat anybody in the United States any time.'

Now at this, Horsey gets right up and steps over to the table and bows and smiles in a friendly way on one and all, and says:

'Gentlemen,' he says, 'pardon the interruption, and excuse me for coming in, but,' he says, 'do I understand you are speaking of a great eater who lives in your fair city?'

Well, these Boston characters all gaze at Horsey in such a hostile manner that I am expecting any one of them to get up and request him to let them miss him, but he keeps on bowing and smiling, and they can see that he is a gentleman, and finally one of them says:

'Yes,' he says, 'we are speaking of a character by the name of Joel Duffle. He is without doubt the greatest eater alive. He just wins a unique deal. He bets a character from Bangor, Me, that he can eat a whole window display of oysters in this very restaurant, and he not only eats all the oysters but he then wishes to bet that

42

e can also eat the shells, but,' he says, 'it seems that the character rom Bangor, Me, unfortunately faints on the first proposal and as nothing with which to bet on the second.'

'Very interesting,' Horsey says, 'very interesting, if true, but,' he says, 'unless my ears deceive me, I hear one of you state that he s willing to wager ten thousand dollars on this eater of yours against anybody in the United States.'

'Your ears are perfect,' another of the Boston characters says. 'I state it, although,' he says, 'I admit it is a sort of figure of speech. But I state it all right,' he says, 'and never let it be said that a Conway ever turns back on a betting proposal.'

'Well,' Horsey says, 'I do not have that kind of money on me at the moment, but,' he says, 'I have here a thousand dollars to put up as a sign that I can produce a character who will outeat your party for ten thousand, and as much more as you care to put up.'

And with this, Horsey outs with a bundle of coarse notes and tosses it on the table, and right away one of the Boston characters, whose name turns out to be Carroll, slaps his hand on the money and says:

'Bet.'

Well, now this is prompt action to be sure, and if there is one thing I admire more than anything else, it is action, and I can see that these are characters of true sporting instincts and I begin wondering where I can raise some money to take a piece of Horsey's proposal, because of course I know that he has nobody in mind to do the eating for his side but Nicely-Nicely Jones.

And knowing Nicely-Nicely Jones, I am prepared to wager all the money I can possibly raise that he can outeat anything that walks on two legs. In fact, I will take a chance on Nicely-Nicely against anything on four legs, except maybe an elephant, and at that he may give the elephant a photo finish.

I do not say that Nicely-Nicely is the greatest eater in all history, but what I do say is he belongs up there as a contender. In fact, Professor D, who is a professor in a college out West before he turns to betting on horses for a living, and who makes a study of

43

history in his time, says he will not be surprised if Nicely-Nicely turns out successful in the end.

Professor D says we must always remember that Nicely-Nicely eats under the handicaps of modern civilization, which require that an eater use a knife and fork, or anyway a knife, while in the old days eating with the hands was a popular custom and much faster. Professor D says he has no doubt that under the old rule Nicely-Nicely will hang up a record that will endure through the ages, but of course maybe Professor D exaggerates somewhat.

Well, now that the match is agreed upon, naturally Horsey and the Boston characters begin discussing where it is to take place, and one of the Boston characters suggests a neutral ground, such as New London, Connecticut, or Providence, Rhode Island, but Horsey wants New York, and it seems that Boston characters are always ready to visit New York, so he does not meet with any great opposition on this point.

They all agree on a date four weeks later so as to give the principals plenty of time to get ready, although Horsey and I know that this is really unnecessary as far as Nicely-Nicely is concerned, because one thing about him is he is always in condition to eat.

This Nicely-Nicely Jones is a character who is maybe five feet eight inches tall, and about five feet nine inches wide, and when he is in good shape he will weigh upward of two hundred and eighty-three pounds. He is a horse-better by trade, and eating is really just a hobby, but he is undoubtedly a wonderful eater even when he is not hungry.

Well, as soon as Horsey and I return to New York, we hasten to Mindy's restaurant and tell about the bet Horsey makes in Boston, and right away so many citizens, including Mindy himself, wish to take a piece of the proposal that it is oversubscribed by a large sum in no time.

Then Mindy remarks that he does not see Nicely-Nicely Jones for a month of Sundays, and then everybody present remembers that they do not see Nicely-Nicely around lately, either, and this leads to a discussion of where Nicely-Nicely can be, although up

44

o this moment if nobody sees Nicely-Nicely but once in the next
en years it will be considered sufficient.

Well, Willie the Worrier, who is a bookmaker by trade, is
among those present, and he remembers that the last time he looks
or Nicely-Nicely hoping to collect a debt of some years past,
Nicely-Nicely is living at the Rest Hotel in West Forty-Ninth
Street, and nothing will do Horsey but I must go with him over to
he Rest to make inquiry for Nicely-Nicely, and there we learn
hat he leaves a forwarding address away up on Morningside
Heights in care of somebody by the name of Slocum.

So away we go to this address, which turns out to be a five-
storey apartment, and a card downstairs shows that Slocum lives
on the top floor. It takes Horsey and me ten minutes to walk up
the five flights as we are by no means accustomed to exercise of
this nature, and when we finally reach a door marked Slocum, we
are completely worn out, and have to sit down on the top step and
rest a while.

Then I ring the bell at this door marked Slocum, and who
appears but a tall young lady with black hair who is without doubt
beautiful, but she is so skinny that we have to look twice to see her,
and when I ask her if she can give me any information about a
party named Nicely-Nicely, she says to me like this:

'I guess you mean Quentin,' she says. 'Yes,' she says, 'Quentin
is here. Come in, gentlemen.'

So we step into an apartment, and as we do so a thin, sickly-
looking character gets up out of a chair by the window, and in a
weak voice says good evening. It is a good evening, at that, so
Horsey and I say good evening right back at him, very polite, and
then we stand there waiting for Nicely-Nicely to appear, when the
beautiful skinny young lady says:

'Well,' she says, 'this is Mr Quentin Jones.'

Then Horsey and I take another look at the thin character, and
we can see that it is nobody but Nicely-Nicely, at that, but the
way he changes since we last observe him is practically shocking to
us both, because he is undoubtedly all shrunk up. In fact, he looks
as if he is about half what he is in his prime, and his face is pale and

45

thin, and his eyes are away back in his head, and while we both shake hands with him it is time before either of us is able to speak. Then Horsey finally says:

'Nicely,' he says, 'can we have a few words with you in private on a very important proposal?'

Well, at this, and before Nicely-Nicely can answer yes or no, the beautiful skinny young lady goes out of the room and slams a door behind her, and Nicely-Nicely says:

'My fiancee, Miss Hilda Slocum,' he says. 'She is a wonderful character. We are to be married as soon as I lose twenty pounds more. It will take a couple of weeks longer,' he says.

'My goodness gracious, Nicely,' Horsey says. 'What do you mean lose twenty pounds more? You are practically skin and bone now. Are you just out of a sick bed, or what?'

'Why,' Nicely-Nicely says, 'certainly I am not out of a sick bed. I am never healthier in my life. I am on a diet. I lose eighty-three pounds in two months, and am now down to two hundred. I feel great,' he says. 'It is all because of my fiancee, Miss Hilda Slocum. She rescues me from gluttony, or anyway,' Nicely-Nicely says, 'this is what Miss Hilda Slocum calls it. My, I feel good. I love Miss Hilda Slocum very much,' Nicely-Nicely says. 'It is a case of love at first sight on both sides the day we meet in the subway. I am wedged in one of the gates, and she kindly pushes on me from behind until I wiggle through. I can see she has a kind heart so I make a date with her for a movie that night and propose to her while the newsreel is on. But,' Nicely-Nicely says, 'Hilda tells me at once that she will never marry a fat chap. She says I must put myself in her hands and she will reduce me by scientific methods and then she will become my ever-loving wife, but not before.

'So,' Nicely-Nicely says, 'I come to live here with Miss Hilda Slocum and her mother, so she can watch my diet. Her mother is thinner than Hilda. And I surely feel great,' Nicely-Nicely says. 'Look,' he says.

And with this, he pulls out the waistband of his pants, and shows enough spare space to hide a man in, but the effort seems to be a strain on him, and he has to sit down in his chair again.

46

'My goodness gracious,' Horsey says. 'What do you eat, Nicely?'

'Well,' Nicely-Nicely says, 'I eat anything that does not contain starch, but,' he says, 'of course everything worth eating contains starch, so I really do not eat much of anything whatever. My fiancee, Miss Hilda Slocum, arranges my diet. She is an expert dietician and runs a widely known department in a diet magazine by the name of Let's Keep House.'

Then Horsey tells Nicely-Nicely of how he is matched to eat against this Joel Duffle, of Boston, for a nice bet, and how he has given a thousand dollars already for the appearance, and how many of Nicely-Nicely's admirers along Broadway are looking to win themselves out of all their troubles by betting on him, and at first Nicely-Nicely listens with great interest, and his eyes are like shining coins, but then he becomes very sad, and says:

'It is no use, gentlemen,' he says. 'My fiancee, Miss Hilda Slocum, will never hear of me going off my diet even for a little while. Only yesterday I try to talk her into letting me have a little extra instead of toasted whole wheat bread, and she says if I even think of such a thing again, she will break our engagement. Horsey,' he says, 'do you ever eat toasted whole wheat bread for a month running? Toasted?' he says.

'No,' Horsey says. 'What I eat is nice, white French bread, and corn muffins, and hot biscuits with gravy on them.'

'Stop,' Nicely-Nicely says. 'You are eating yourself into an early grave, and furthermore,' he says, 'you are breaking my heart. But,' he says, 'the more I think of my following depending on me in this emergency, the sadder it makes me feel to think I am unable to oblige them. However,' he says, 'let us call Miss Hilda Slocum in on an outside chance and see what her reactions to your proposal are.'

So we call Miss Hilda Slocum in, and Horsey explains our problem in putting so much faith in Nicely-Nicely only to find him dieting, and Miss Hilda Slocum's reactions are to order Horsey and me out of the place with instructions never to darken her door again, and when we are a block away we can still hear her voice speaking very firmly to Nicely-Nicely.

47

Well, personally, I figure this ends the matter, for I can see th. Miss Hilda Slocum is a most determined character indeed, and tl chances are it does end it, at that, if Horsey does not happen to g a wonderful break of luck.

He is at Belmont Park one afternoon, and he has a real goo thing in a jump race, and when a brisk young character in a har straw hat and eyeglasses comes along and asks him what he like Horsey mentions this good thing, figuring he will move himse! in for a useful profit if the good thing connects.

Well, it connects all right, and the brisk young character is ver grateful to Horsey for his information, and is giving him plenty o much-obliges, and nothing else, and Horsey is about to mentior that they do not accept much-obliges at his hotel, when the bris! young character mentions that he is nobody but Mr McBurgl and that he is the editor of the Let's Keep House magazine, an. for Horsey to drop in and see him any time he is around his way

Naturally, Horsey remembers what Nicely-Nicely says abou Miss Hilda Slocum working for this Let's Keep House magazine and he tells the story of the eating contest to Mr. McBurgle anc asks him if he will kindly use his influence with Miss Hilda Slocum to get her to release Nicely-Nicely from his diet long enough for the contest. Then Horsey gives Mr McBurgle a tip or another winner for the race, and Mr McBurgle must use plenty of influence on Miss Hilda Slocum at once, as the next day she calls Horsey up at his hotel before he is out of bed, and speaks to him as follows:

'Of course,' Miss Hilda Slocum says, 'I will never change my attitude about Quentin, but,' she says, 'I can understand that he feels very bad about you gentlemen relying on him and having to disappoint you. He feels that he lets you down, which is by no means true, but it weighs upon his mind. It is interfering with his diet.

'Now,' Miss Hilda Slocum says, 'I do not approve of your contest, because,' she says, 'it is placing an emphasis on gluttony, but I have a friend by the name of Miss Violette Shumberger who may answer your purpose. She is my dearest friend from childhood, ut it is only because I love her dearly that this friendship endures. he is extremely fond of eating,' Miss Hilda Slocum says. 'In spite f my pleadings, and my warnings, and my own example, she persts in food. It is disgusting to me but I finally learn that it is no se arguing with her.

'She remains my dearest friend,' Miss Hilda Slocum says, though she continues her practice of eating, and I am informed hat she is remarkable in this respect. In fact,' she says, 'Nicely-Nicely tells me to say to you that if Miss Violette Shumberger can perform the eating exploits I tell him from hearsay she is the woman for you. Good-bye,' Miss Hilda Slocum says, 'you cannot save Nicely-Nicely.'

Well, nobody cares much about this idea of a stand-in for Nicely-Nicely in such a situation, and especially a woman that no one ever hears of before, and many citizens are in favour of pulling out of the contest altogether. But Horsey has his one thousand dollars to think of, and as no one can suggest anyone else, he finally arranges a personal meet with the lady suggested by Miss Hilda Slocum.

He comes into Mindy's one evening with a female character who s so fat it is necessary to push three tables together to give her room for her lap, and it seems that this character is Miss Violette Shumberger. She weighs maybe two hundred and fifty pounds, but she is by no means an old woman, and by no means bad-looking. She has a face the size of a town clock and enough chins for a fire escape, but she has a nice smile and pretty teeth, and a laugh that is so hearty it knocks the cream off an order of strawberry cake on a table fifty feet away and arouses the indignation of a customer by the name of Goldstein who is about to eat same.

Well, Horsey's idea in bringing her into Mindy's is to get some kind of idea on her eating form, and she is clocked by many experts when she really starts eating, and it is agreed by one and all that she is by no means a poor competitor. In fact, by the time she gets through, even Mindy admits she has plenty of class, and the result of it all is Miss Violette Shumberger is chosen to eat against Joel Duffle.

49

Maybe you hear something of this great eating contest that comes off in New York one night in the early summer of 1937. Of course eating contests are by no means anything new, and in fact they are quite an old-fashioned game in some sections of the country, such as the South and East, but this is the first big public contest of the kind in years, and it creates no little comment along Broadway.

In fact, there is some mention of it in the papers, and it is not a frivolous proposal in any respect, and more money is wagered on it than any other eating contest in history, with Joel Duffle a 6 to favourite over Miss Violette Shumberger all the way through.

This Joel Duffle comes to New York several days before the contest with a character by the name of Conway, and requests a meet with Miss Violette Shumberger to agree on the final details and who shows up with Miss Violette Shumberger as her coach and adviser but Nicely-Nicely Jones. He is even thinner and more ill-looking than when Horsey and I see him last, but he says he feels great, and that he is within six pounds of his marriage to Miss Hilda Slocum.

Well, it seems that his presence is really due to Miss Hilda Slocum herself, because she says that after getting her dearest friend Miss Violette Shumberger into this game, it is only fair to do all she can to help her win it, and the only way she can think of is to let Nicely-Nicely give Violette the benefit of his experience and advice.

But afterwards we learn that what really happens is that this editor, Mr McBurgle, gets greatly interested in the contest, and when he discovers that in spite of his influence, Miss Hilda Slocum refuses to permit Nicely-Nicely to personally compete, but puts in a substitute, he is quite indignant and insists on her letting Nicely-Nicely school her.

Furthermore we afterward learn that when Nicely-Nicely returns to the apartment on Morningside Heights after giving Violette a lesson, Miss Hilda Slocum always smells his breath to see if he has taken any food during his absence.

Well, this Joel Duffle is a tall character with stooped shoulders,

nd a sad expression, and he does not look as if he can eat his way
ut of a tea shop, but as soon as he commences to discuss the
etails of the contest, anybody can see that he knows the form in
tuations such as this. In fact, Nicely-Nicely says he can tell at
nce from the way Joel Duffle talks that he is a dangerous opponent,
nd he says while Miss Shumberger impresses him as an improv-
ng eater, he is only sorry she does not have more seasoning.

This Joel Duffle suggests that the contest consist of twelve
ourses of strictly American food, each side to be allowed to pick
x dishes, doing the picking one after the other, and naming the
eight and quantity of the course selected to any amount the con-
estant making the pick desires, and each course is to be divided
or eating exactly in half, and after Miss Violette Shumberger and
Nicely-Nicely whisper together a while, they say the terms are
uite satisfactory.

Then Horsey tosses a coin for the first pick, and Joel Duffle says
eads, and it is heads, and he chooses, as the first course, two
uarts of ripe olives, twelve bunches of celery, and four pounds of
helled nuts, all this to be split equally between them. Miss Violette
Shumberger names twelve dozen clams, as the second course, and
oel Duffle says two gallons of Philadelphia pepper-pot soup as the
hird.

Well, Miss Violette Shumberger and Nicely-Nicely whisper
ogether again, and Violette puts in two five-pound fish, the heads
nd tails not to count in the eating, and Joel Duffle names a
wenty-two pound roast turkey. Each vegetable is known as one
ourse, and Miss Violette Shumberger asks for twelve pounds of
mashed potatoes with brown gravy. Joel Duffle says two dozen
ears of corn, and Violette replies with two quarts of beans. Joel
Duffle calls for twelve bunches of asparagus cooked in butter, and
Violette mentions ten pounds of stewed new peas.

This gets them down to the salad, and it is Joel Duffle's play, so
he says six pounds of mixed green salad with vinegar and oil dress-
ng, and now Miss Violette Shumberger has the final selection,
which is the dessert. She says it is a pumpkin pie, two feet across,
and not less than three inches deep.

It is agreed they must eat with knife, fork or spoon, but speed not to count, and there is to be no time limit, except they cann[ot] pause more than two consecutive minutes at any stage, except i[n] case of hiccoughs. They can drink anything, and as much as the[y] please, but liquids are not to count in the scoring. The decision [is] to be strictly on the amount of food eaten, and the judges are [to] take account of anything left on the plates after a course, but not [of] food accidentally dropped—up to an ounce. The losing side is t[o] pay for the food, and in case of a tie they are to eat it off immediatel[y] on ham and eggs only.

Well, the scene of this contest is the second-floor dining-room o[f] Mindy's restaurant, which is closed to the general public for th[e] occasion, and only parties immediately concerned in the contes[t] are admitted. The contestants are seated on either side of a bi[g] table in the centre of the room, and each contestant has thre[e] waiters.

No talking from the spectators is permitted, but of course in an eating contest the principals may speak to each other if they wis[h] though smart eaters never wish to do this, as talking only waste[s] energy, and about all they ever say to each other is please pass th[e] mustard.

About fifty characters from Boston are present to witness th[e] contest, and the same number of citizens of New York are ad[-] mitted, and among them is this editor, Mr McBurgle, and he i[s] around asking Horsey if he thinks Miss Violette Shumberger is a[s] good a thing as the jumper at the race track.

Nicely-Nicely arrives on the scene quite early, and his appear[-] ance is really most distressing to his old friends and admirers, a[s] by this time he is without so much weight that he is a pitiful scene[,] to be sure, but he tells Horsey and me that he thinks Miss Violett[e] Shumberger has a good chance.

'Of course,' he says, 'she is green. She does not know how t[o] control her speed in competition. But,' he says, 'she has a wonder[-] ful style. I love to watch her eat. She likes the same things I do i[n] the days when I am eating. She is a wonderful character, too. D[o] you ever notice her smile?' Nicely-Nicely says.

'But,' he says, 'she is the dearest friend of my fiancee, Miss Hilda Slocum, so let us not speak of this. I try to get Hilda to come see the contest, but she says it is dreadful. Well, anyway,' Nicely-Nicely says, 'I manage to borrow a few dollars, and am wagering on Miss Violette Shumberger. By the way,' he says, 'if you happen to think of it, notice her smile.'

Well, Nicely-Nicely takes a chair about ten feet behind Miss Violette Shumberger, which is as close as the judges will allow him, and he is warned by them that no coaching from the corners will be permitted, but of course Nicely-Nicely knows this rule as well as they do, and furthermore by this time his efforts seem to have left him without any more energy.

There are three judges, and they are all from neutral territory. One of these judges is a party from Baltimore by the name of Packard, who runs a restaurant, and another is a party from Providence by the name of Croppers, who is a sausage manufacturer. The third judge is an old woman by the name of Mrs. Rhubarb, who comes from Philadelphia, and once keeps an actors' boarding-house, and is considered an excellent judge of eaters.

Well, Mindy is the official starter, and at 8.30 p.m. sharp, when there is still much betting among the spectators, he outs with his watch, and says like this:

'Are you ready, Boston? Are you ready, New York?'

Miss Violette Shumberger and Joel Duffle both nod their heads, and Mindy says commence, and the contest is on, with Joel Duffle getting the jump at once on the celery and olives and nuts.

It is apparent that this Joel Duffle is one of these rough eaters that you can hear quite a distance off, especially on clams and soups. He is also an eyebrow eater, an eater whose eyebrows go up as high as the part in his hair as he eats, and this type of eater is undoubtedly very efficient.

In fact, the way Joel Duffle goes through the groceries down to the turkey causes the Broadway spectators some uneasiness, and they are whispering to each other that they only wish the old Nicely-Nicely is in there. But personally, I like the way Miss Violette Shumberger eats without undue excitement, and with great zest.

53

She cannot keep close to Joel Duffle in the matter of speed in th early stages of the contest, as she seems to enjoy chewing her foo but I observe as it goes along she draws nearer to him, and I figu this is not because she is getting quicker, but because he is slowir down.

When the turkey finally comes on, and is split in two halv right down the middle, Miss Violette Shumberger looks great disappointed, and she speaks for the first time as follows:

'Why,' she says, 'where is the stuffing?'

Well, it seems that nobody mentions any stuffing for the turke to the cook, so he does not make any stuffing, and Miss Violet Shumberger's disappointment is so plain to be seen that the cor fidence of the Boston characters is somewhat shaken. They can se that a woman who can pack away as much food as Miss Violett Shumberger has so far, and then demand stuffing, is really quite a eater.

In fact, Joel Duffle looks quite startled when he observes Mi Violette Shumberger's disappointment, and he gazes at her wit great respect as she disposes of her share of the turkey, and th mashed potatoes, and one thing and another in such a manner tha she moves up on the pumpkin pie on dead even terms with hin In fact, there is little to choose between them at this poin although the judge from Baltimore is calling the attention of th other judges to a turkey leg that he claims Miss Violette Shum berger does not clean as neatly as Joel Duffle does his, but th other judges dismiss this as a small thing.

Then the waiters bring on the pumpkin pie, and it is withou doubt quite a large pie, and in fact it is about the size of a sma table top, and I can see that Joel Duffle is observing this pie with strange expression on his face, although to tell the truth I do no care for the expression on Miss Violette Shumberger's face eithe

Well, the pie is cut in two dead centre, and one half is place before Miss Violette Shumberger and the other half before Joe Duffle, and he does not take more than two bites before I see hir loosen his waistband and take a big drink of water, and thinks I t myself, he is now down to a slow walk, and the pie will decide th

whole match, and I am only wishing I am able to wager a litt
more money on Miss Violette Shumberger. But about this momen
and before she as much as touches her pie, all of a sudden Violet
turns her head and motions to Nicely-Nicely to approach her, an
as he approaches, she whispers in his ear.

Now at this, the Boston character by the name of Conway jum
up and claims a foul and several other Boston characters join hi
in this claim, and so does Joel Duffle, although afterwards even th
Boston characters admit that Joel Duffle is no gentleman to mak
such a claim against a lady.

Well, there is some confusion over this, and the judges hold
conference, and they rule that there is certainly no foul in th
actual eating that they can see, because Miss Violette Shumberge
does not touch her pie so far.

But they say that whether it is a foul otherwise all depends o
whether Miss Violette Shumberger is requesting advice on th
contest from Nicely-Nicely and the judge from Providence wishe
to know if Nicely-Nicely will kindly tell what passes between hin
and Violette so they may make a decision.

'Why,' Nicely-Nicely says, 'all she asks me is can I get he
another piece of pie when she finishes the one in front of her.'

Now at this, Joel Duffle throws down his knife, and pushes bac
his plate with all but two bites of his pie left on it, and says to th
Boston characters like this:

'Gentlemen,' he says, 'I am beaten. I cannot eat anothe
mouthful. You must admit I put up a good battle, but,' he says, 'i
is useless for me to go on against this woman who is asking fo
more pie before she even starts on what is before her. I am almos
dying as it is, and I do not wish to destroy myself in a hopeles
effort. Gentlemen,' he says, 'she is not human.'

Well, of course this amounts to a victory for the other side, anc
Nicely-Nicely stands up on his chair, and says:

'Three cheers for Miss Violette Shumberger!'

Then Nicely-Nicely gives the first cheer in person, but the
effort overtaxes his strength, and he falls off the chair in a fain'
just as Joel Duffle collapses under the table, and the doctors at the

56

ospital are greatly puzzled to receive, from the same address at
e same time, one patient who is suffering from undernourish-
ent, and another patient who is unconscious from over-eating.

Well, in the meantime, after the excitement dies down, and
agers are settled, we take Miss Violette Shumberger to the main
oor in Mindy's for a midnight snack, and when she speaks of her
onderful triumph, she is inclined to give much credit to Nicely-
icely Jones.

'You see,' Violette says, 'what I really whisper to him is that I
n finished. I whisper to him that I cannot possibly take one bite
the pie if my life depends on it, and if he has any bets on me to
y and get rid of them as quickly as possible.

'I fear,' she says, 'that Nicely-Nicely will be greatly disappointed
my showing, but I have a confession to make to him when he
ts out of the hospital. I forget about the contest,' Violette says,
nd eat my regular dinner an hour before the contest starts and,'
ae says, 'I have no doubt this tends to affect my form some-
hat. So,' she says, 'I owe everything to Nicely-Nicely's quick
ainking.'

It is several weeks after the great eating contest that I run into
liss Hilda Slocum on Broadway and it seems to me that she looks
auch better than the last time I see her, and when I mention this
ae says:

'Yes,' she says, 'I cease dieting. I learn my lesson,' she says. 'I
arn that male characters do not appreciate anybody who tries to
et rid of extra fat. What male characters wish is substance. Why,'
ae says, 'only a week ago my editor, Mr McBurgle, tells me he
ill love to take me dancing if only I get something on me for him
o take hold of. I am very fond of dancing,' she says.

'But,' I say, 'what of Nicely-Nicely Jones? I do not see him
round lately.'

'Why,' Miss Hilda Slocum says, 'do you not hear what this
hap does? Why, as soon as he is strong enough to leave the hos-
ital, he goes off with my dearest friend, Miss Violette Shum-
erger, leaving me with a note saying something about two souls
ith but a single thought. They are down in Florida running a

restaurant, and,' she says, 'the chances are, eating like seve
horses.'

'Miss Slocum,' I says, 'can I interest you in a portion of Mindy
special chicken?'

'With dumplings?' Miss Hilda Slocum says. 'Yes,' she say
'you can. Afterwards I have a date to go dancing with M
McBurgle. I am crazy about dancing,' she says.

The Night the Ghost
Got In

JAMES THURBER

James Thurber (1894–1961) was humorist, wit, poet, illus-
trator and short-story writer. Indeed many of his short
stories combine these skills in a small space and show him
at his best—making fun of our complicated modern life.
Two of his most enjoyable collections are *My World and
Welcome to It*, and *My Life and Hard Times* from which
the present story is taken. He also wrote two excellent
modern fairy tales: *The Magnificent O* and *The Thirteen
Clocks*.

THE ghost that got into our house on the night of November 17,
1915, raised such a hullabaloo of misunderstandings that I am
sorry that I didn't just let it keep on walking, and go to bed. Its
coming caused my mother to throw a shoe through a window of
the house next door and ended up with my grandfather shooting a
patrolman. I am sorry, therefore, as I have said, that I ever paid
any attention to the footsteps.

They began about a quarter past one o'clock in the morning, a
rhythmic, quick kind of walk around the dining-room table. My
mother was asleep in one room upstairs, my brother Herman in
another; grandfather was in the attic, in the old bed which, as you
will remember, once fell on my father. I had just stepped out of
the bathtub and was busily rubbing myself with a towel when I
heard the steps. They were the steps of a man walking rapidly
around the dining-room table downstairs. The light from the
bathroom shone down the back steps, which dropped directly into

the dining-room; I could see the faint shine of plates on the plate
rail; I couldn't see the table. The steps kept going round an
round the table; at regular intervals a board creaked, when it wa
trod upon. I supposed at first that it was my father or my brothe
Roy, who had gone to Indianapolis but were expected home a
any time. I suspected next that it was a burglar. It did not enter m
mind until later that it was a ghost.

After the walking had gone on for perhaps three minutes, I tip
toed to Herman's room. 'Psst!' I hissed, in the dark, shaking him
'Awp,' he said, in the low, hopeless tone of a very sad bird—h
always half suspected that something would 'get him' in the night
I told him who I was. 'There's something downstairs!' I said. H
got up and followed me to the head of the back staircase. W
listened together. There was no sound. The steps had ceased
Herman looked at me in some alarm: I had only the bath towe
around my waist. He wanted to go back to bed, but I gripped hi
arm. 'There's something down there!' I said. Instantly the step
began again, circled the dining-room table like a man running, an
started up the stairs towards us, heavily, two at a time. The ligh
still shone palely down to the stairs; we saw nothing coming; w
only heard the steps. Herman rushed to his room and slammed th
door. I slammed shut the door at the stairs top and held my kne
against it. After a long minute, I slowly opened it again. There wa
nothing there. There was no sound. None of us ever heard th
ghost again.

The slamming of the doors had awakened mother: she peere
out of her room. 'What on earth are you boys doing?' she de
manded. Herman came nervously out of his room. 'Nothing,' h
said, secretly, but he was, in colour, a light green. 'What was al
that running around downstairs?' said mother. So she had hear
the steps, too! We just looked at her. 'Burglars!' she shouted b
instinct. I tried to quiet her by starting lightly downstairs.

'Come on, Herman,' I said.

'I'll stay with mother,' he said. 'She's all excited.'

'Don't either of you go a step,' said mother. 'We'll call th
police.' Since the phone was downstairs, I didn't see how we were

60

oing to call the police—nor did I want the police—but mother made one of her quick, remarkable decisions. She flung up a window of her bedroom, which faced the bedroom windows of the house of a neighbour, picked up a shoe, and threw it straight through a pane of glass across the narrow space that separated the two houses. Glass tinkled into the bedroom occupied by a retired man named Bodwell and his wife. Bodwell had been for some years in rather a bad way and was subject to mild 'attacks' of illness. Almost everybody we knew or lived near had *some* kind of attacks.

It was now about two o'clock of a moonless night; clouds hung black and low. Bodwell was at the window in a minute, shouting, frothing a little, shaking his fist. 'We'll sell the house and go back to Peoria,' we could hear Mrs Bodwell saying. It was some time before mother 'got through' to Bodwell. 'Burglars!' she shouted. 'Burglars in the house!' Herman and I hadn't dared to tell her that it was not burglars but ghosts, for she was even more afraid of ghosts than of burglars. Bodwell at first thought that she meant there were burglars in his house, but finally he quieted down and called the police for us over an extension telephone by his bed. After he had disappeared from the window, mother suddenly made as if to throw another shoe, not because there was further need of it but, as she later explained, because the thrill of throwing a shoe through a glass window had enormously taken her fancy. I prevented her.

The police were at hand in an excellently short time: a Ford car full of them, two on motor cycles, and a patrol wagon with about eight in it and a few reporters. They began banging at our front door. Torches flashed up and down the walls, across the yard, down the walk between our house and Bodwell's. 'Open up!' cried a voice. 'We're men from Headquarters!' I wanted to go down and let them in, since there they were, but mother wouldn't hear of it. 'You'd catch your death of cold.' I wound the towel around me again. Finally the police put their shoulders to our heavy front door with its thick glass and broke it in: I could hear a breaking of wood and a splash of glass on the floor of the hall. Their lights played all over the living-room and crossed nervously in the dining-

room, shone into hallways, shot up the front stairs and finally u
the back. They caught me standing in my towel at the top.
heavy policeman jumped up the steps. 'Who are you?' he de
manded. 'I live here,' I said. 'Well, what's a matter, ya hot?' h
asked. It was, as a matter of fact, cold; I went to my room an
pulled on some trousers. On my way out, a cop stuck a gun into m
ribs. 'Whatta you doin' here?' he demanded. 'I live here,' I said

The officer in charge reported to mother. 'No sign of nobod
lady,' he said. 'Must've got away—whatt'd he look like?' 'The
were two or three of them,' mother said, 'shouting all over th
place and slamming doors. 'Funny,' said the cop. 'All ya window
and doors were locked on the inside tight as a grave.'

Downstairs, we could hear the tramping of the other polic
Police were all over the place; doors were pulled open, drawe
were pulled open, windows were shot up and pulled dow
furniture fell with dull thumps. A half-dozen policemen came ou
of the darkness of the front hallway upstairs. They began to ran
sack the floor: pulled beds away from walls, tore clothes out of th
cupboards, pulled suitcases and boxes off shelves. One of the
found an old zither that Roy had won in a game. 'Looky here
Joe,' he said playing it with a big paw. The cop named Joe took
and turned it over. 'What is it?' he asked me. 'It's an old zithe
our pig used to sleep on,' I said. It was true that a pet pig that w
once had would never sleep anywhere except on the zither, but
should never have said so. Joe and the other cop looked at me for
long time. They put the zither back on a shelf.

'No sign o' nuthin',' said the cop who had first spoken t
mother. 'This chap,' he explained to the others, pushing a thum
at me, 'was naked. The lady seems historical.'[1] They all nodded
but said nothing; just looked at me. In the small silence we a
heard a creaking in the attic. Grandfather was turning over in bed
'What's 'at?' snapped Joe. Five or six cops sprang for the atti
door before I could explain. I realised that it would be bad if they
burst in on grandfather unannounced, or even announced. He wa

[1] Historical: wrongly used for 'hysterical' or state in which one's feel
ings cannot be controlled.

62

oing through a period in which he believed that General Meade's
men, under steady attack by Stonewall Jackson, were beginning
to retreat and even give up.

When I got to the attic, things were pretty confused. Grandfather had evidently jumped to the conclusion that the police were
in fact running away from Meade's army, trying to hide in his
attic. He jumped out of bed wearing a long nightgown over his
long woollen underwear, a nightcap, and a leather jacket around
his chest. The cops must have realized at once that the indignant,
white-haired old man belonged in the house, but they had no
chance to say so. 'Back, ye cowardly dogs!' roared grandfather.
Back t' the lines, ye goddam lily-livered cattle!' With that, he
gave the officer who found the zither a flat-handed blow alongside
his head that sent him down to the ground. The others quickly
made a retreat, but not fast enough; grandfather caught hold of
Zither's gun and let fly. The report seemed to crack the roof;
smoke filled the attic. A cop cursed and shot his hand to his
shoulder. Somehow, we all finally got downstairs again and locked
the door against the old gentleman. He fired once or twice more
in the darkness and then went back to bed. 'That was grandfather,'
I explained to Joe, out of breath. 'He thinks you're running away
from the army.' 'I'll say he does,' said Joe.

The cops were unwilling to leave without getting their hands on
somebody besides grandfather; the night had been distinctly a
defeat for them. Furthermore, they obviously didn't like the 'lay-
out'; something looked—and I can see their viewpoint—phony.
They began to look into things again. A reporter, a thin-faced man,
came up to me. I had put on one of mother's blouses, not being
able to find anything else. The reporter looked at me with mixed
suspicion and interest. 'Just what the hell has been going on down
here, Bud?' he asked. I decided to be frank with him. 'We had
ghosts,' I said. He gazed at me a long time as if I were a machine
into which he had, without results, dropped a coin. Then he walked
away. The cops followed him, the one grandfather shot holding

is now-bandaged arm, cursing like mad. 'I'm gonna get my gun
back from that old bird,' said the zither-cop. 'Yeh,' said Joe. 'You
—and who else?' I told them I would bring it to the station house
the next day.

'What was the matter with that one policeman?' mother asked,
after they had gone. 'Grandfather shot him,' I said. 'What for?'
he demanded. I told her he was a deserter. 'Of all things!' said
mother. 'He was such a nice-looking young man.'

Grandfather was fresh as a daisy and full of jokes at breakfast
next morning. We thought at first he had forgotten all about what
had happened, but he hadn't. Over his third cup of coffee, he
glared at Herman and me. 'What was the idea of all them cops
runnin' round the house last night?' he demanded. He beat us there,
all right.

The Killers

ERNEST HEMINGWAY

Ernest Hemingway (1898–1961) has been the most popular and universally known of American writers in the first
half of the twentieth century. His finest novels are *A Farewell to Arms*, *For Whom the Bell Tolls*, and *The Old Man
and the Sea* and deal with love, war, and deep-sea fishing,
three of the subjects that Hemingway wrote most carefully
about. His stories have had a remarkable influence through
their plain active language, and *The Killers* is typical. He
was awarded the Nobel Prize for Literature in 1954.

One should remember in reading Hemingway that he is
skilful at representing uneducated speech. This means
that many of the expressions used, such as 'don't he', 'he
never even seen us', 'I got to', etc., are not acceptable as
good British or American English, and should not be
copied in students' work.

THE door of Henry's lunch-room opened and two men came in.
They sat down at the counter.

'What's yours?' George asked them.

'I don't know,' one of the men said. 'What do you want to eat,
Al?'

'I don't know,' said Al. 'I don't know what I want to eat.'

Outside it was getting dark. The street light came on outside the
window. The two men at the counter read the menu. From the
other end of the counter Nick Adams watched them. He had been
talking to George when they came in.

'I'll have some roast pork with apple sauce and mashed potatoes,'
the first man said.

66

'It isn't ready yet.'

'What the hell do you put it on the card for?'

'That's the dinner,' George explained. 'You can get that at six 'clock.'

George looked at the clock on the wall behind the counter.

'It's five o'clock.'

'The clock says twenty minutes past five,' the second man said.

'It's twenty minutes fast.'

'Oh, to hell with the clock,' the first man said. 'What have you ot to eat?'

'I can give you any kind of sandwiches,' George said. 'You can ave ham and eggs, bacon and eggs, liver and bacon, or a steak.'

'Give me chicken with green peas and cream sauce and mashed otatoes.'

'That's the dinner.'

'Everything we want's the dinner, eh? That's the way you work t.'

'I can give you ham and eggs, bacon and eggs, liver—'

'I'll take ham and eggs,' the man called Al said. He wore a hat nd a black overcoat buttoned across his chest. His face was small nd white and he had tight lips. He wore a silk scarf and gloves.

'Give me bacon and eggs,' said the other man. He was about the ame size as Al. Their faces were different, but they were dressed like twins. Both wore overcoats too tight for them. They sat leaning forward, their elbows on the counter.

'Got anything to drink?' Al asked.

'Light beer, orange, ginger-ale,' George said.

'I meant you got anything to *drink*?'

'Just those I said.'

'This is a hot town,' said the other. 'What do they call it?'

'Summit.'

'Ever hear of it?' Al asked his friend.

'No,' said the friend.

'What do you do here, nights?' Al asked.

'They eat the dinner,' his friend said. 'They all come here and eat the big dinner.'

67

'That's right,' George said.

'So you think that's right?' Al asked George.

'Sure.'

'You're a pretty bright boy, aren't you?'

'Sure,' said George.

'Well, you're not,' said the other little man. 'Is he, Al?'

'He's dumb,' said Al. He turned to Nick. 'What's your name?'

'Adams.'

'Another bright boy,' Al said. 'Ain't he a bright boy, Max?'

'The town's full of bright boys,' Max said.

George put down two plates, one of ham and eggs, the other of bacon and eggs, on the counter. He set down two side dishes of fried potatoes and closed the gate into the kitchen.

'Which is yours?' he asked Al.

'Don't you remember?'

'Ham and eggs.'

'Just a bright boy,' Max said. He leaned forward and took the ham and eggs. Both men ate with their gloves on. George watched them eat.

'What are *you* looking at?' Max looked at George.

'Nothing.'

'The hell you were. You were looking at me.'

'Maybe the boy meant it for a joke, Max,' Al said.

George laughed.

'*You* don't have to laugh,' Max said to him. '*You* don't have to laugh at all, see?'

'All right,' said George.

'So he thinks it's all right,' Max turned to Al. 'He thinks it's all right. That's a good one.'

'Oh, he's a thinker,' Al said. They went on eating.

'What's the bright boy's name down the counter?' Al asked Max.

'Hey, bright boy,' Max said to Nick. 'You go around on the other side of the counter with your boy friend.'

'What's the idea?' Nick asked.

'There isn't any idea.'

68

'You better go around, bright boy,' Al said. Nick went around behind the counter.

'What's the idea?' George asked.

'None of your damn business,' Al said. 'Who's out in the kitchen?'

'The nigger.'

'What do you mean the nigger?'

'The nigger that cooks.'

'Tell him to come in.'

'What's the idea?'

'Tell him to come in.'

'Where do you think you are?'

'We know damn well where we are,' the man called Max said. 'Do we look silly?'

'You talk silly,' Al said to him. 'What the hell do you argue with this kid for? Listen,' he said to George, 'tell the nigger to come out here.'

'What are you going to do to him?'

'Nothing. Use your head, bright boy. What would we do to a nigger?'

George opened the hatch that opened back into the kitchen. 'Sam,' he called. 'Come in here for a minute.'

The door of the kitchen opened and the nigger came in. 'What was it?' he asked. The two men at the counter took a look at him.

'All right, nigger. You stand right there,' Al said.

Sam, the nigger, standing in his apron, looked at the two men sitting at the counter. 'Yes, sir,' he said. Al got down from his stool.

'I'm going back to the kitchen with the nigger and bright boy,' he said. 'Go back to the kitchen, nigger. You go with him, bright boy.' The little man walked after Nick and Sam, the cook, back into the kitchen. The door shut after them. The man called Max sat at the counter opposite George. He didn't look at George but looked in the mirror that ran along back of the counter. Henry's had been made over from a saloon into a lunch-counter.

70

'Well, bright boy,' Max said, looking into the mirror, 'why on't you say something?'

'What's it all about?'

'Hey, Al,' Max called, 'bright boy wants to know what it's all bout.'

'Why don't you tell him?' Al's voice came from the kitchen.

'What do you think it's all about?'

'I don't know.'

'What do you think?'

Max looked into the mirror all the time he was talking.

'I wouldn't say.'

'Hey, Al, bright boy says he wouldn't say what he thinks it's all bout.'

'I can hear you, all right,' Al said from the kitchen. He had ushed open the hatch that dishes passed through into the kitchen vith a bottle. 'Listen, bright boy,' he said from the kitchen to George. 'Stand a little further along the bar. You move a little to he left, Max.' He was like a photographer arranging for a group picture.

'Talk to me, bright boy,' Max said. 'What do you think's going o happen?'

George did not say anything.

'I'll tell you,' Max said. 'We're going to kill a Swede. Do you know a big Swede named Ole Andreson?'

'Yes.'

'He comes in here to eat every night, don't he?'

'Sometimes he comes here.'

'He comes here at six o'clock, don't he?'

'If he comes.'

'We know all that, bright boy,' Max said. 'Talk about something else. Ever go to the movies?'

'Once in a while.'

'You ought to go to the movies more. The movies are fine for a bright boy like you.'

'What are you going to kill Ole Andreson for? What did he ever do to you?'

71

'He never had a chance to do anything to us. He never eve[n] seen us.'

'And he's only going to see us once,' Al said from the kitchen.

'What are you going to kill him for, then?' George asked.

'We're killing him for a friend. Just to oblige a friend, brigh[t] boy.'

'Shut up,' said Al from the kitchen. 'You talk too goddam[n] much.'

'Well, I got to keep bright boy amused. Don't I, bright boy?'

'You talk too damn much,' Al said. 'The nigger and my brigh[t] boy are amused by themselves. I got them tied up like a couple o[f] girl friends in the convent.'

'I suppose you were in a convent.'

'You never know.'

'You were in a Jewish convent. That's what you were.'

George looked up at the clock.

'If anybody comes in you tell them that the cook is off, and i[f] they keep after it, you tell them you'll go back and cook yourself[.] Do you get that, bright boy?'

'All right,' George said. 'What are you going to do with us afterwards?'

'That'll depend,' Max said. 'That's one of those things you[ ] never know at the time.'

George looked up at the clock. It was a quarter past six. The[ ] door from the street opened. A street-car motorman came in.

'Hello, George,' he said. 'Can I get supper?'

'Sam's gone out,' George said. 'He'll be back in about half an hour.'

'I'd better go up the street,' the motorman said. George looked at the clock. It was twenty minutes past six.

'That was nice, bright boy,' Max said. 'You're a regular little gentleman.'

'He knew I'd blow his head off,' Al said from the kitchen.

'No,' said Max. 'It ain't that. Bright boy is nice. He's a nice boy. I like him.'

At six-fifty-five George said: 'He's not coming.'

72

Two other people had been in the lunch-room. Once George had gone out to the kitchen and made a ham-and-egg sandwich that a man wanted to take with him. Inside the kitchen he saw Al, his hat pushed back, sitting on a stool beside the hatch with a sawed-off shotgun resting on the ledge. Nick and the cook were back to back in the corner, a towel tied in each of their mouths. George had cooked the sandwich, wrapped it up in oiled paper, put it in a bag, and the man had paid for it and gone out.

'Bright boy can do everything,' Max said. 'He can cook and everything. You'd make some girl a nice wife, bright boy.'

'Yes?' George said. 'Your friend, Ole Andreson, isn't going to come.'

'We'll give him ten minutes,' Max said.

Max watched the mirror and the clock. The hands of the clock marked seven o'clock, and then five minutes past seven.

'Come on, Al,' said Max. 'We better go. He's not coming.'

'Better give him five minutes,' Al said from the kitchen.

In the five minutes a man came in, and George explained that the cook was sick.

'Why the hell don't you get another cook?' the man asked. 'Aren't you running a lunch-counter?' He went out.

'Come on, Al,' Max said.

'What about the two bright boys and the nigger?'

'They're all right.'

'You think so?'

'Sure. We're through with it.'

'I don't like it,' said Al. 'It's sloppy. You talk too much.'

'Oh, what the hell,' said Max. 'We got to keep amused, haven't we?'

'You talk too much, all the same,' Al said. He came out from the kitchen. The cut-off barrels of the shotgun made a slight bulge under the waist of his too tight-fitting overcoat. He straightened his coat with his gloved hands.

'So long, bright boy,' he said to George. 'You got a lot of luck.'

'That's the truth,' Max said. 'You ought to play the races, bright boy.'

73

The two of them went out of the door. George watched them through the window, pass under the lights, and cross the street. In their tight overcoats and hats they looked like a team of comedy performers. George went back through the swinging-door into the kitchen and untied Nick and the cook.

'I don't want any more of that,' said Sam, the cook. 'I don' want any more of that.'

Nick stood up. He had never had a towel in his mouth before.

'Say,' he said. 'What the hell?' He was trying to swagger it off.

'They were going to kill Ole Andreson,' George said. 'They were going to shoot him when he came in to eat.'

'Ole Andreson?'

'Sure.'

The cook felt the corners of his mouth with his thumbs.

'They all gone?' he asked.

'Yeah,' said George. 'They're gone now.'

'I don't like it,' said the cook. 'I don't like any of it at all.'

'Listen,' George said to Nick. 'You better go see Ole Andreson.'

'All right.'

'You better not have anything to do with it at all,' Sam, the cook, said. 'You'd better keep right away from it.'

'Don't go if you don't want to,' George said.

'Mixing up in this ain't going to get you anywhere,' the cook said. 'You stay out of it.'

'I'll go and see him,' Nick said to George. 'Where does he live?'

The cook turned away.

'Little boys always know what they want to do,' he said.

'He lives up at Hirsch's rooming-house,' George said to Nick.

Outside, the lights shone through the bare branches of a tree. Nick walked up the street and turned at the next light down a side-street. Three houses up the street was Hirsch's rooming-house. Nick walked up the two steps and pushed the bell. A woman came to the door.

'Is Ole Andreson here?'

'Do you want to see him?'

74

'Yes, if he's in.'

Nick followed the woman up a flight of stairs and back to the end of the corridor. She knocked on the door.

'Who is it?'

'It's somebody to see you, Mr Andreson,' the woman said.

'It's Nick Adams.'

'Come in.'

Nick opened the door and went into the room. Ole Andreson was lying on the bed with all his clothes on. He had been a heavy-weight prize-fighter and he was too long for the bed. He lay with his head on two pillows. He did not look at Nick.

'What was it?' he asked.

'I was up at Henry's,' Nick said, 'and two fellows came in and tied me up and the cook, and they said they were going to kill you.'

It sounded silly when he said it. Ole Andreson said nothing.

'They put us out in the kitchen,' Nick went on. 'They were going to shoot you when you came in to supper.'

Ole Andreson looked at the wall and did not say anything.

'George thought I'd better come and tell you about it.'

'There isn't anything I can do about it,' Ole Andreson said.

'I'll tell you what they were like.'

'I don't want to know what they were like,' Ole Andreson said. He looked at the wall. 'Thanks for coming to tell me about it.'

'That's all right.'

Nick looked at the big man lying on the bed.

'Don't you want me to go and see the police?'

'No,' Ole Andreson said. 'That wouldn't do any good.'

'Isn't there something I could do?'

'No. There ain't anything to do.'

'Maybe it was just a bluff.'

'No. It ain't a bluff.'

Ole Andreson rolled over towards the wall.

'The only thing is,' he said, talking towards the wall, 'I just can't make up my mind to go out. I been in here all day.'

'Couldn't you get out of town?'

'No,' Ole Andreson said. 'I'm through with all that running around.'

He looked at the wall.

'There ain't anything to do now.'

'Couldn't you fix it up in some way?'

'No. I've done the wrong things.' He talked in the same flat voice. 'There ain't anything to do. After a while I'll make up my mind to go out.'

'I better go back and see George,' Nick said.

'So long,' said Ole Andreson. He did not look towards Nick. 'Thanks for coming around.'

Nick went out. As he shut the door he saw Ole Andreson with all his clothes on, lying on the bed looking at the wall.

'He's been in his room all day,' the landlady said downstairs. 'I guess he don't feel well. I said to him: "Mr Andreson, you ought to go out and take a walk on a nice fall day like this," but he didn't feel like it.'

'He doesn't want to go out.'

'I'm sorry he don't feel well,' the woman said. 'He's an awfully nice man. He was in the ring, you know.'

'I know it.'

'You'd never know it except from the appearance of his face,' the woman said. They stood talking just inside the street door. 'He's just as gentle.'

'Well, good-night, Mrs Hirsch,' Nick said.

'I'm not Mrs Hirsch,' the woman said. 'She owns the place. I just look after it for her. I'm Mrs Bell.'

'Well, good-night, Mrs Bell,' Nick said.

'Good-night,' the woman said.

Nick walked up the dark street to the corner under the lamplight, and then along by the road to Henry's eating-house. George was inside, back of the counter.

'Did you see Ole?'

'Yes,' said Nick. 'He's in his room and he won't go out.'

The cook opened the door from the kitchen when he heard Nick's voice.

'I don't even listen to it,' he said and shut the door.

'Did you tell him about it?' George asked.

'Sure. I told him, but he knows what it's all about.'

'What's he going to do?'

'Nothing.'

'They'll kill him.'

'I guess they will.'

'He must have got mixed up in something in Chicago.'

'I guess so,' said Nick.

'It's a hell of a thing.'

'It's an awful thing,' Nick said.

They did not say anything. George reached down for a towel and wiped the counter.

'I wonder what he did?' Nick said.

'Double-crossed somebody. That's what they kill them for.'

'I'm going to get out of this town,' Nick said.

'Yes,' said George. 'That's a good thing to do.'

'I can't stand to think about him waiting in the room and knowing he's going to get it. It's too damned awful.'

'Well,' said George, 'you better not think about it.'

The Open Boat

STEPHEN CRANE

With Stephen Crane (1871–1900) modern American
literature began. He was one of the first to search for the
truth in a manner that succeeding writers have found right
and sympathetic for the twentieth century. His life was
brief and restless and included experience of wars in Cuba
and Greece as well as wide travel in his own country.
Despite his energy, Crane did not write much that has
permanent value except for two works: a novel, *The Red
Badge of Courage* about war, and a short story, *The Open
Boat* about the sea. The story is a most convincing account
of courage and danger. It is based on an actual event in
Crane's life.

I

NONE of them knew the colour of the sky. Their eyes glanced
level, and were fastened upon the waves that swept towards them.
These waves were of the colour of slate, except for the tops, which
were white, and all of the men knew the colours of the sea. The
horizon narrowed and widened, and dipped and rose, and at all
times its edge was fierce with waves that seemed to push up in
points like rocks.

Many a man ought to have a bathtub larger than the boat which
here rode upon the sea. These waves were most wrongfully abrupt
and tall, and each was a problem in small-boat navigation.

The cook sat in the bottom, and looked with both eyes at the
six inches of gunwale which separated him from the ocean. His
sleeves were rolled over his fat arms, and the two edges of his
unbuttoned vest hung loose as he bent to bail out the boat. Often

said, 'Gawd! that was a near miss!' As he said it he always
gazed eastward over the broken sea.

The oiler, steering with one of the two oars in the boat, sometimes raised himself suddenly to keep clear of water that came in
over the stern. It was a thin little oar, and it seemed often ready to
break.

The correspondent, pulling at the other oar, watched the waves
and wondered why he was there.

The injured captain, lying in the bow, was at this time buried in
that deep misery and carelessness which comes, temporarily at
least, to even the bravest when, whether they like it or not, the
business fails, the army loses, the ship goes down. The mind of
the master of a vessel is rooted deep in the wood of her, though he
command for a day or a year.

'Keep 'er a little more south, Billie,' said he.

'A little more south, sir,' said the oiler in the stern.

In the pale light the faces of the men must have been grey. Their
eyes must have shone in strange ways as they gazed steadily astern.
The sun swung steadily up the sky, and they knew it was broad
day because the colour of the sea changed from slate to green
touched with orange lights, and the foam was like snow. The pro-
cess of the breaking day was unknown to them. They were aware
only of this effect upon the colour of the waves that rolled towards
them.

In disconnected sentences the cook and the correspondent
argued as to the difference between a life-saving station and a
house of refuge. The cook had said: 'There's a house of refuge
just north of the Mosquito Inlet Light, and as soon as they see us
they'll come off in their boat and pick us up.'

'As soon as who sees us?' said the correspondent.

'The crew,' said the cook.

'Houses of refuge don't have crews,' said the correspondent. 'As
I understand them, they are only places where clothes and food
are stored for the benefit of shipwrecked people. They don't carry
crews.'

'Oh, yes, they do,' said the cook.

'No, they don't,' said the correspondent.

'Well, we're not there yet, anyhow,' said the oiler, in the stern.

'Well,' said the cook, 'perhaps it's not a house of refuge that I'm thinking of as being near Mosquito Inlet Light; perhaps it's a life saving station.'

'We're not there yet,' said the oiler in the stern.

II

As the boat bounced from the top of each wave the wind tore through the hair of the hatless men, and as the craft rose and fell, giving them a broad view with every wave, the waters flew past them. It was probably splendid, it was probably glorious, this play of the free sea, wild with lights of green and white and yellow.

'Jolly good thing it's an on-shore wind,' said the cook. 'If not, where would we be? Wouldn't have a show.'

'That's right,' said the correspondent.

The busy oiler agreed.

Then the captain, in the bow, chuckled in a way that expressed humour and tragedy in one. 'Do you think we've got much of a show now, boys?' said he.

At which the three were silent, thinking their hopes.

'Oh, well,' said the captain, calming his children, 'we'll get ashore all right.'

But there was that in his tone which made them think; so the oiler said, 'Yes! if this wind keeps on.'

The cook was bailing. 'Yes! if we don't catch hell in the surf.'

In the meantime the oiler and the correspondent rowed. And also they rowed. They sat together in the same seat, and each rowed an oar. Then the oiler took both oars; then the correspondent took both oars; then the oiler; then the correspondent. They rowed and rowed. The very difficult part of the business was when the time came for the one in the stern to take his turn at the oars. By the very last star of truth, it is easier to steal the eggs from under a hen than it was to change seats in this boat. First the man in the stern slid his hand along the seat and moved with care, as if

e were breakable. Then the man in the rowing seat slid his hand
long. It was all done with the most extraordinary care. As the two
ent past each other, the whole party kept watchful eyes on the
oming wave, and the captain cried: 'Look out, now! Steady,
here!'

The captain, standing carefully in the bow after the boat had
sen on a great wave, said that he had seen the lighthouse at Mos-
uito Inlet. Presently the cook remarked that he had seen it. The
orrespondent was at the oars then, and for some reason he too
ished to look at the lighthouse; but his back was towards the far
hore, and the waves were important, and for some time he could
ot seize an opportunity to turn his head. But at last there came a
ave more gentle than the others, and when at the top of it he
wiftly searched the western horizon.

'See it?' said the captain.

'No,' said the correspondent, slowly; 'I didn't see anything.'

'Look again,' said the captain. He pointed. 'It's exactly in that
irection.'

At the top of another wave the correspondent did as he was told,
nd this time his eyes caught a small, still thing on the edge of the
noving horizon. It was precisely like the point of a pin. It took an
nxious eye to find a lighthouse so tiny.

'Think we'll get there, Captain?'

'If this wind keeps on and the boat don't sink, we can't do much
lse,' said the captain.

'Bail her, cook,' said the captain, serenely.

'All right, Captain,' said the cheerful cook.

III

It would be difficult to describe the subtle brotherhood of men
hat was here established on the seas. No one said that it was so.
No one mentioned it. But it dwelt in the boat, and each man felt it
warm him. They were a captain, an oiler, a cook, and a correspondent, and they were friends—friends in a more curiously iron-
bound degree than may be common. The hurt captain, lying
against the water-jar in the bow, spoke always in a low voice and

calmly; but he could never command a more ready and swift obedient crew than the odd three of this boat. It was more than recognition of what was best for the common safety. There wa surely in it a quality that was personal and heart-felt. And aft this devotion to the commander of the boat, there was this com radeship, that the correspondent, for instance, who had bee taught to be cynical of men, knew even at the time was the be: experience of his life. But no one said that it was so. No one men tioned it.

Meanwhile the lighthouse had been growing slowly larger. I now almost had colour, and appeared like a little grey shadow o the sky. The man at the oars could not be prevented from turnin his head rather often to try for a glimpse of this little gre shadow.

At last, from the top of each wave, the men in the tossing boa could see land. Even as the lighthouse was an upright shadow o the sky, this land seemed but a long black shadow on the sea. I certainly was thinner than paper. 'We must be about opposite Nev Smyrna,' said the cook, who had coasted this shore often i schooners. 'Captain, by the way, I believe they abandoned tha life-saving station there about a year ago.'

'Did they?' said the captain.

The wind slowly died away.

Slowly the land arose from the sea. From a black line it became line of black and a line of white—trees and sand. Finally the cap tain said that he could make out a house on the shore. 'That's th house of refuge, sure,' said the cook. 'They'll see us before long and come out after us.'

The distant lighthouse stood up high. 'The keeper ought to b able to make us out now, if he's looking through a glass,' said th captain. 'He'll warn the life-saving people.'

'None of those other boats could have got ashore to give word o this wreck,' said the oiler, in a low voice, 'else the life-boat woul be out hunting us.'

Slowly and beautifully the land came out of the sea. The wind came again. It had changed from the north-east to the south-east

inally a new sound struck the ears of the men in the boat. It was
ue low thunder of the surf on the shore. 'We'll never be able to
uake the lighthouse now,' said the captain. 'Swing her head a little
more north, Billie.'

'A little more north, sir,' said the oiler.

Whereupon the little boat turned her nose once more down the
und, and all but the oarsman watched the shore grow. As this
appened, doubt was leaving the minds of the men. The manage-
ent of the boat was still most absorbing, but it could not prevent
quiet cheerfulness. In an hour, perhaps, they would be ashore.

Their backbones had become thoroughly used to balancing in
ue boat, and they now rode this wild horse of a craft like experts.
he correspondent thought that he had been wet to the skin, but
uppening to feel in the top pocket of his coat, he found therein
ght cigars. Four of them were soaked with sea-water; four were
erfectly dry. After a search, somebody produced three dry
uatches; and thereupon the four homeless ones rode impudently
u their little boat and, with the feeling of an early rescue shining
u their eyes, puffed at the big cigars, and judged well and ill of all
uen. Everybody took a drink of water.

IV

'Cook,' remarked the captain, 'there don't seem to be any signs
f life about your house of refuge.'

'No,' replied the cook. 'Funny they don't see us.'

A broad stretch of lowly coast lay before the eyes of the men. It
as of low hills topped with dark vegetation. The roar of the surf
as plain, and sometimes they could see the white lip of a wave as
came up the beach. A tiny house was blocked out black upon the
ky. Southward, the thin lighthouse lifted its little grey length.

Tide, wind and waves were swinging the boat northward.
Funny they don't see us,' said the men. The surf's roar was here
ulled, but its tone was nevertheless thunderous and mighty. As
he boat swam over the great rollers the men sat listening to this
oar. 'We'll swamp sure,' said everybody.

It is fair to say here that there was not a life-saving station with-

in twenty miles in either direction; but the men did not know th
fact, and in consequence they made dark remarks concerning t
eyesight of the nation's life-savers. Four angry men sat in the boa
swearing.

'Funny they don't see us.'

The light-heartedness of a former time had completely fade
To their sharpened minds it was easy to invent pictures of a
kinds of inefficiency and blindness and, indeed, cowardice. The
was the shore of the crowded land, and it was bitter and bitter
them that from it came no sign.

'Well,' said the captain, at last, 'I suppose we'll have to make
try for ourselves. If we stay out here too long, we'll none of us ha
strength left to swim after the boat swamps.'

And so the oiler, who was at the oars, turned the boat straig
for the shore. There was a sudden tightening of muscles. The
was some thinking.

'If we don't all get ashore,' said the captain—'if we don't all g
ashore, I suppose you fellows know where to send news of m
finish?'

They then briefly exchanged addresses and advice. As for th
thoughts of the men, there was a great deal of rage in them. Pe
haps they might be expressed thus: 'If I am going to be drowned–
if I am going to be drowned—if I am going to be drowned, wh
in the name of the seven mad gods who rule the sea, was I allowe
to come thus far and gaze at the sand and trees? Was I broug
here merely to have my nose dragged away as I was about to nibb
the sacred cheese of life? It is preposterous. If this old woma
Fate, cannot do better than this, she should be deprived of th
management of men's fortunes. She is an old hen who knows n
her intention. If she has decided to drown me, why did she not d
it at the beginning and save me all this trouble? The whole affair
absurd. But no; she cannot mean to drown me. She dare not drow
me. She cannot drown me. Not after all this work.' Afterward th
man might have had an impulse to shake his fist at the cloud
'Just you drown me, now; and then hear what I call you!'

The waves that came at this time were even greater. The

emed always just about to break and roll over the little boat in a adness of foam. There was a long growl in the speech of them. o mind unused to the sea would have concluded that the boat uld climb these heights in time. The shore was still afar. The ler was a cunning surfman. 'Boys,' he said swiftly, 'she won't ve three minutes more, and we're too far out to swim. Shall I ke her to sea again, Captain?'

'Yes; go ahead!' said the captain.

The oiler, by a series of quick miracles and fast and steady arsmanship, turned the boat in the middle of the surf and took er safely to sea again.

There was a considerable silence as the boat rocked over the sea deeper water. Then somebody in low spirits spoke: 'Well, any-ow, they must have seen us from the shore by now.'

'Look! There's a man on the shore!'

'Where?'

'There! See 'im? See 'im?'

'Yes, sure! He's walking along.'

'Now he's stopped. Look! He's facing us!'

'He's waving at us!'

'So he is! By thunder!'

'Ah, now we're all right! Now we're all right! There'll be a boat ut here for us in half an hour.'

'He's going on. He's running. He's going up to that house there.'

The distant beach seemed lower than the sea, and it required a earching glance to see the little black figure. The captain saw a oating stick, and they rowed to it. A bath towel was by some trange chance in the boat, and, tying this on the stick, the captain raved it. The oarsman did not dare turn his head, so he was bliged to ask questions.

'What's he doing now?'

'He's standing still again. He's looking, I think.—There he oes again—toward the house.—Now he's stopped again.'

'Is he waving at us?'

'No, not now; he was, though.'

'Look! There comes another man!'

'He's running.'

'Look at him go, would you!'

'Why, he's on a bicycle. Now he's met the other man. They're both waving at us. Look!'

'There comes something up the beach.'

'What the devil is that thing?'

'Why, it looks like a boat.'

'Why, certainly, it's a boat.'

'No; it's on wheels.'

'Yes, so it is. Well, that must be the life-boat. They drag them along shore on a wagon.'

'That's the life-boat, sure.'

'No, by God, it's—it's a bus.'

'I tell you it's a life-boat.'

'It is not! It's a bus. I can see it plain. See? One of these big hotel buses.'

'By thunder, you're right. It's a bus, sure as fate. What do you suppose they are doing with a bus? Maybe they are going around collecting the life-crew, hey?'

'That's it, likely. Look! There's a fellow waving a little black flag. He's standing on the steps of the bus. There come those other two fellows. Now they're all talking together. Look at the fellow with the flag. Maybe he ain't waving it!'

'That ain't a flag, is it? That's his coat. Why, certainly, that's his coat.'

'So it is; it's his coat. He's taken it off and is waving it around his head. But would you look at him swing it!'

'Oh, say, there isn't any life-saving station there. That's just a hotel bus that has brought over some of the tourists to see us drown.'

'What's that idiot with the coat mean? What's he signalling, anyhow?'

'It looks as if he were trying to tell us to go north. There must be a life-saving station up there.'

'No; he thinks we're fishing. Just giving us a merry hand. See? Ah, there, Willie!'

'Well, I wish I could make something out of those signal. What do you suppose he means?'

'He don't mean anything; he's just playing.'

'Well, if he'd just signal us to try the surf again, or to go to se and wait, or go north, or go south, or go to hell, there would k some reason in it. But look at him! He just stands there and keep his coat turning like a wheel. The ass!'

'There come more people.'

'Now there's quite a crowd. Look! Isn't that a boat?'

'Where? Oh, I see where you mean. No, that's no boat.'

'That fellow is still waving his coat.'

'He must think we like to see him do that. Why don't he stop i It don't mean anything.'

'I don't know. I think he is trying to make us go north. It mu be that there's a life-saving station there somewhere.'

'Say, he ain't tired yet. Look at him wave!'

'Wonder how long he can keep that up. He's been turning h coat ever since he caught sight of us. He's an idiot. Why aren't the getting men to bring a boat out? A fishing-boat—one of those bi things—could come out here all right. Why don't he do some thing?'

'Oh, it's all right now.'

'They'll have a boat out here for us in less than no time, no that they've seen us.'

A faint yellow tone came into the sky over the low land. Th shadows on the sea slowly deepened. The wind bore coldness wit it, and the men began to shiver.

'Holy smoke!' said one, allowing his voice to express hi irritation, 'if we keep on messing about out here! If we've got t stay out here all night!'

'Oh, we'll never have to stay here all night! Don't you worry They've seen us now, and it won't be long before they'll com chasing out after us.'

The shore grew dark. The man waving a coat disappeare gradually, and in the same manner the dark swallowed the bu and the group of people.

'I'd like to catch the ass who waved the coat. I feel like hitting m one, just for luck.'

'Why? What did he do?'

'Oh, nothing, but then he seemed so damned cheerful.'

In the meantime the oiler rowed, and then the correspondent wed, and then the oiler rowed. Grey-faced and bowed forward, ey mechanically, turn by turn, worked the leaden oars. The rm of the lighthouse had vanished from the southern horizon, it finally a pale star appeared, just lifting from the sea. The llow in the west passed before the all-conquering darkness, and e sea to the east was black. The land had vanished, and was pressed only by the low and sad thunder of the surf.

'If I am going to be drowned—if I am going to be drowned—if im going to be drowned, why, in the name of the seven mad gods ho rule the sea, was I allowed to come thus far and look at sand d trees? Was I brought here only to have my nose dragged away I was about to nibble the sacred cheese of life?'

The patient captain, lying over the water-jar, was sometimes >liged to speak to the oarsman.

'Keep her head up! Keep her head up!'

'Keep her head up, sir.' The voices were weary and low.

This was surely a quiet evening. All save the oarsman lay :avily and tiredly in the boat's bottom. As for him, his eyes were st capable of noting the tall black waves that swept forward in a ost sinister silence, save for an occasional noise of a crest.

The cook's head was on a seat, and he looked without interest at e water under his nose. He was deep in other scenes. Finally he >oke. 'Billie,' he murmured, dreamfully, 'what kind of pie do >u like best?'

'Pie!' said the oiler and the correspondent, nervously. 'Don't lk about those things, blast you!'

'Well,' said the cook, 'I was just thinking about ham sand-iches and —'

A night on the sea in an open boat is a long night. As darkness :ttled finally, the shine of the light, lifting from the sea in the >uth, changed to full gold. On the northern horizon a new light

89

appeared, a small bluish gleam on the edge of the waters. The
two lights were the furniture of the world. Otherwise there w
nothing but waves.

In a low voice the correspondent addressed the captain. He w
not sure that the captain was awake, although this iron man seem
to be always awake. 'Captain, shall I keep her making for th
light north, sir?'

The same steady voice answered him. 'Yes. Keep it about tv
points off the port bow.'

The cook had tied a life-belt around himself in order to get ev
the warmth which this awkward thing could give, and he seem
just about stove-like when a rower, whose teeth almost alwa
chattered wildly as soon as he ceased his labour, dropped down
sleep.

The correspondent, as he rowed, looked down at the two m
sleeping underfoot. The cook's arm was around the oiler
shoulders, and, with their ragged clothing and thin faces, th
were like children, lost in a boat at sea.

Later he must have grown stupid at his work, for sudden
there was a growling of water, and a crest came with a roar into th
boat, and it was a wonder that it did not set the cook afloat in l
life-belt. The cook continued to sleep, but the oiler sat up, blin
ing his eyes and shaking with the new cold.

'Oh, I'm awfully sorry, Billie,' said the correspondent.

'That's all right, old boy,' said the oiler, and lay down again a
was asleep.

Presently it seemed that even the captain dozed, and th
correspondent thought that he was the one man afloat on all th
oceans. The wind had a voice as it came over the waves, and it w
sadder than the end.

There was a long, loud noise astern of the boat, and a gleamir
trail of phosphorescence, like blue flame, was marked on the blac
waters. It might have been made by a terrible knife.

Then there came a stillness, while the correspondent breathe
with open mouth and looked at the sea.

Suddenly there was another sound and another long flash

luish light, and this time it was alongside the boat, and might most have been reached with an oar. The correspondent saw a uge fin speed like a shadow through the water, throwing the iamond-like spray and leaving the long glowing trail.

The correspondent looked over his shoulder at the captain. His ace was hidden, and he seemed to be asleep. He looked at the abes of the sea. They certainly were asleep. So, being without ympathy, he leaned a little way to one side and swore softly into he sea.

But the thing did not then leave the area of the boat. Ahead or stern, on one side or the other, at intervals long or short, fled the ong shining line, and there was to be heard the faint sound of the ark fin. The speed and power of the thing was greatly to be dmired. It cut the water like a vast, keen bullet.

The presence of this thing did not affect the man with the same orror that it would if he had been a tourist. He simply looked at he sea dully and swore softly.

Nevertheless, it is true that he did not wish to be alone with the hing. He wished one of his companions to awake by chance and eep him company with it. But the captain hung motionless over he water-jar, and the oiler and the cook in the bottom of the boat vere plunged in sleep.

VI

'If I am going to be drowned—if I am going to be drowned—if am going to be drowned, why, in the name of the seven mad gods vho rule the sea, was I allowed to come thus far and look at sand nd trees?'

During this awful night, it may be remarked that a man would onclude that it was really the intention of the seven mad gods to lrown him, despite the abominable injustice of it. For it was cerainly an abominable injustice to drown a man who had worked so aard, so hard. The man felt it would be a crime most unnatural. Other people had drowned at sea since ships sailed with painted ails, but still —

A high cold star on a winter's night is the only word he feels the

world has to say to him. Thereafter he knows the sadness of h
situation.

Agreeing with his emotion, a verse mysteriously entered th
correspondent's head. He had even forgotten that he had fo
gotten this verse, but it suddenly was in his mind.

'A soldier of the Legion lay dying in Algiers;
    There was lack of woman's nursing, there was dearth of
        woman's tears;
    But a comrade stood beside him, and he took that comrade'
        hand,
    And he said, "I never more shall see my own, my native
        land".'

In his childhood the correspondent had been made acquainte
with the fact that a soldier of the Legion lay dying in Algiers, bu
he had never regarded the fact as important. Many of his school
fellows had informed him of the soldier's situation, but this ha
naturally ended by making him perfectly uninterested. He ha
never considered it his affair that a soldier of the Legion lay dyin
in Algiers, nor had it appeared to him as a matter for sorrow. I
was less to him than the breaking of a pencil's point.

Now, however, it suddenly came to him as a human, living thing
It was no longer merely a picture of a few feelings in the breast o
a poet, meanwhile drinking tea and warming his feet at the hearth
it was an actuality—stern, mournful, and fine.

The correspondent plainly saw the soldier. He lay on the san
with his feet out straight and still. While his pale left hand wa
upon his chest in an attempt to stop the going of his life, the bloo
came between his fingers. In the far Algerian distance, a city o
low square forms was set against a sky that was faint with the las
sunset colours. The correspondent, working the oars and dream
ing of the slow and slower movements of the lips of the soldier
was moved by a profound and perfectly impersonal understanding
He was sorry for the soldier of the Legion who lay dying in Algiers

The thing which had followed the boat and waited had evidentl
grown bored at the delay. There was no longer to be heard th

92

ound of the water, and there was no longer the flame of the long
rail. The light in the north still shone, but it was apparently no
nearer to the boat. Sometimes the cry of the surf rang in the
correspondent's ears, and he turned the craft seaward then and
rowed harder. Southward, someone had evidently built a watch-
re on the beach. It was too low and too far to be seen, but it made
dancing, half-red reflection upon the cliff at the back of it, and
this could be seen from the boat. The wind came stronger, and
sometimes a wave suddenly raged out like a mountain cat, and
there was to be seen the brightness of a broken crest.

The captain, in the bow, moved on his water-jar and sat up.
'Pretty long night,' he observed to the correspondent. He looked
at the shore. 'Those life-saving people take their time.'

'Did you see that shark playing around?'

'Yes, I saw him. He was a big fellow, all right.'

'Wish I had known you were awake.'

Later the correspondent spoke into the bottom of the boat.
'Billie!' There was a slow and gradual movement. 'Billie, will you
take over?'

'Sure,' said the oiler.

As soon as the correspondent touched the cold, comfortable sea-
water in the bottom of the boat and had got close to the cook's life-
belt he was deep in sleep, despite the fact that his teeth played all
the popular airs. This sleep was so good to him that it was but a
moment before he heard a voice call his name in a tone that had in
it the last stages of exhaustion.

'Sure, Billie.'

The light in the north had mysteriously vanished, but the
correspondent took his course from the wide-awake captain.

Later in the night they took the boat farther out to sea, and the
captain ordered the cook to take one oar at the stern and keep the
boat facing the seas. He was to call out if he should hear the thunder of the surf. This plan allowed the oiler and the correspondent
to get a rest at the same time. 'We'll give those boys a chance to
get into shape again,' said the captain. They lay down, and after a
word or two, slept once more the dead sleep. Neither knew they

93

had left to the cook the company of another shark, or perhaps the same shark.

As the boat rocked on the waves, spray occasionally came over the side and gave them a fresh wetting, but this had no power to break their rest. The threatening sound of the wind and the water affected them as it would have affected spirits.

'Boys,' said the cook, with the notes of every unwillingness in his voice, 'she's drifted in pretty close. I guess one of you had better take her to sea again.' The correspondent, waking up, heard the crash of the falling crests.

As he was rowing, the captain gave him some whisky-and-water, and this steadied the chills out of him. 'If I ever get ashore and anybody shows me even a photograph of an oar —'

At last there was a short conversation.

'Billie!—Billie, will you take over?'

'Sure,' said the oiler.

VII

When the correspondent again opened his eyes, the sea and the sky were each of the grey colour of the dawning. Later, red and gold was painted upon the waters. The morning appeared finally in its splendour, with a sky of pure blue, and the sunlight flamed on the tops of the waves.

On the distant sands were set many little black cottages, and a tall white windmill stood above them. No man, nor dog, nor bicycle appeared on the beach. The cottages might have formed a deserted village.

The voyagers searched the shore. A conference was held in the boat. 'Well,' said the captain, 'if no help is coming, we had better try a run through the surf right away. If we stay out here much longer we will be too weak to do anything for ourselves at all.' The others silently agreed in this reasoning.

'Now, boys,' said the captain, 'she is going to swamp sure. All we can do is to work her in as far as possible, and then when she swamps, jump out and try for the beach. Keep cool now, and don't jump until she swamps sure.'

94

The oiler took the oars. Over his shoulders he searched the surf. 'Captain,' he said, 'I think I'd better bring her about and keep her head-on to the seas and back her in.'

'All right, Billie,' said the captain. 'Back her in.' The oiler swung the boat then, and, seated in the stern, the cook and the correspondent were forced to look over their shoulders to see the lonely, careless shore.

At this time there were no hurried words, no faintings, no plain nervousness. The men simply looked at the shore. 'Now, remember to get well clear of the boat when you jump,' said the captain.

Seaward the crest of a wave suddenly fell with a thunderous crash, and the long white waters came roaring down upon the boat.

'Steady now,' said the captain. The men were silent. They turned their eyes from the shore to the wave and waited. The boat slid up the hill, leaped at the angry top, bounced over it, and swung down the long back of the wave. Some water had been taken in, and the cook bailed it out.

But the next crest crashed also. The tumbling, boiling flood of white water caught the boat and twisted it almost perpendicular. Water came in from all sides. The correspondent had his hands on the side of the boat at this time, and when the water entered at this place he swiftly withdrew his fingers, as if he objected to wetting them.

The little boat, drunken with this weight of water, sat more deeply down into the sea.

'Bail her out, cook! Bail her out!' said the captain.

'All right, Captain,' said the cook.

'Now, boys, the next one will end us for sure,' said the oiler. 'Mind to jump clear of the boat.'

The third wave moved forward, huge, furious, irresistible. It fairly swallowed the boat, and almost simultaneously the men tumbled into the sea. A piece of life-belt had lain in the bottom of the boat, and as the correspondent went overboard he held this to his chest with his left hand.

The January water was icy, and he reflected immediately that it was colder than he had expected to find it off the coast of Florida. This appeared to his wandering mind as a fact important enough to be noted at the time. The coldness of the water was sad; it was tragic. This fact was somehow mixed and confused with his opinion of his own situation, so that it seemed almost a proper reason for tears. The water was cold.

When he came to the surface he was conscious of little but the noisy water. Afterwards he saw his companions in the sea. The oiler was ahead in the race. He was swimming strongly and rapidly. Off to the correspondent's left, the cook's great white back stuck out of the water; and in the rear the captain was hanging with his one good hand to the edge of the overturned boat.

There is a certain immovable quality to a shore, and the correspondent wondered at it in the middle of the confusion of the sea.

It seemed also very attractive; but the correspondent knew that it was a long journey, and he went slowly. The piece of the life-belt lay under him, speeding him down the side of a wave from time to time.

But finally he arrived at a place in the sea where travel was difficult. He did not pause swimming to inquire what manner of current had caught him, but there his progress ceased. The shore was set before him like a bit of scenery on a stage, and he looked at it and understood with his eyes each detail of it.

As the cook passed, much farther to the left, the captain was calling to him, 'Turn over on your back, cook! Turn over on your back and use the oar.'

'All right, sir.' The cook turned on his back, and paddling with his oar, went ahead as if he were a canoe.

Presently the boat also passed to the left of the correspondent, with the captain holding on to it with great effort. The correspondent wondered at the captain still being able to manage it.

They passed on nearer to shore—the oiler, the cook, the captain —and following them went the water-jar, bouncing gaily over the seas.

The correspondent remained in the grip of this strange new

nemy—a current. The shore, with its white sand and its green
liff topped with little silent cottages, was spread like a picture
efore him. It was very near to him then, but he was impressed as
ne who, in a gallery, looks at a scene from Brittany or Algiers.

He thought: 'I am going to drown? Can it be possible? Can it
e possible?' Perhaps an individual must consider his own death
o be the final event of nature.

But later a wave perhaps pulled him out of this small deadly
current, for he found suddenly that he could again make progress
owards the shore. Later still he was aware that the captain, holding
n to the boat with one hand, had his face turned away from the
shore and towards him, and was calling his name. 'Come to the
boat! Come to the boat!'

In his struggle to reach the captain and the boat, he reflected
that when one gets properly wearied drowning must really be a
comfortable arrangement—an end to the battle, accompanied by
a large degree of relief; and he was glad of it, for the main thing in
his mind for some moments had been horror of the short agony.
He did not wish to be hurt.

Presently he saw a man running along the shore. He was undressing with most remarkable speed. Coat, trousers, shirt, everything flew magically off him.

'Come to the boat!' called the captain.

'All right, Captain.' As the correspondent paddled, he saw the
captain let himself down to bottom and leave the boat. Then the
correspondent performed his one little marvel of the voyage. A
large wave caught him and flung him with ease and supreme speed
completely over the boat and far beyond it. It struck him even
then as an event in gymnastics and a true miracle of the sea. An
overturned boat in the surf is not a plaything to a swimming man.

The correspondent arrived in water that reached only to his
waist, but his condition did not allow him to stand for more than a
moment. Each wave knocked him down, and the currents pulled
at him.

Then he saw the man who had been running and undressing,
and undressing and running, come jumping into the water. He

97

dragged ashore the cook, and then went towards the captain; bu
the captain waved him away and sent him to the correspondent
He was naked—naked as a tree in winter; but a halo was about hi
head, and he shone like a saint. He gave a strong pull, and a lon
drag at the correspondent's hand. The correspondent, schooled i
this kind of politeness, said, 'Thanks, old man.' But suddenly th
man cried, 'What's that?' He pointed a swift finger. The correspondent said 'Go.'

In the shallows, face downward, lay the oiler. His forehea
touched sand that was periodically, between each wave, clear o
the sea.

The correspondent did not know all that happened afterward.
When he reached safe ground he fell, striking the sand with each
particular part of his body. It was as if he had dropped from a roof,
but the fall was grateful to him.

It seemed that instantly the beach was crowded with men with
blankets, clothes, and flasks, and women with coffee-pots and all
the remedies sacred to their minds. The welcome of the land to
the men from the sea was warm and generous; but a still, wet shape
was carried slowly up the beach, and the land's welcome for it
could only be the different and dreadful hospitality of the grave.

When it came night, the white waves paced to and fro in the
moonlight, and the wind brought the sound of the great sea's
voice to the men on the shore, and they felt that they could then be
interpreters.

The Lady, or The Tiger?

FRANK STOCKTON

Frank Stockton (1834–1902), a wood-engraver by trade
and training, was in his middle forties before he became
well known as an original humorous writer. *Rudder Grange*
and the two novels that continued the story brought him a
large audience, while the publication in 1882 of *The Lady,
or The Tiger?* raised a storm of debate. His most popular
novel was *The Casting Away of Mrs Lecks and Mrs Aleshine*,
a story of shipwreck, and he was also admired for his children's tales. He had a most individual and enjoyable
American talent.

IN the very olden time there lived a half-barbaric king. He was a
man of tremendous fancy, and, also, of an authority so irresistible
that, at his will, he turned his varied fancies into facts. He was
greatly given to meditating with himself; and when he and himself agreed upon anything, the thing was done. So long as all things
moved in their appointed course, he was smooth and gentle; but
if there was a little difficulty and something was not quite right,
he was smoother and more gentle still, for nothing pleased him so
much as to make the crooked straight, and crush down uneven
places.

Among the borrowed ideas by which he spread his barbarism
was that of the public arena, in which, by exhibitions of manly and
horrible courage, the minds of his subjects were refined and cultured.

But even here the tremendous and barbaric fancy showed itself.
The arena of the king was built not to give the people an opportunity of hearing the last words of dying soldiers, nor to allow

them to view the inevitable end of a conflict between religious opinions and hungry jaws, but for purposes far more useful in widening and developing the mental energies of the people. This vast arena was an agent of poetic justice, in which crime was punished, or virtue rewarded, by the commands of an impartial and incorruptible chance.

When a subject was accused of a crime of sufficient importance to interest the king, public notice was given that on an appointed day the fate of the accused person would be decided in the king's arena—a building which well deserved its name; for, although its form and plan were borrowed from afar, its purpose came from this man only, who, every inch a king, knew no tradition to which he owed more faith than pleased his fancy, and who added to every form of human thought and action the rich growth of his barbaric ideas.

When all the people had assembled in the arena, and the king, surrounded by his court, sat high up on his throne of royal state on one side, he gave a signal, a door beneath him opened, and the accused subject stepped out. Directly opposite him, on the other side of the enclosed space, were two doors, exactly alike and side by side. It was the duty and the privilege of the person on trial to walk directly to these doors and open one of them. He could open either door he pleased; he was subject to no guidance or influence but that of the earlier mentioned impartial and incorruptible chance. If he opened the one, there came out of it a hungry tiger, the fiercest and most cruel that could be got, which immediately sprang upon him and tore him to pieces, as a punishment for his guilt. The moment that the case of the criminal was thus decided, sad iron bells were rung, great cries went up from the hired mourners posted on the outer edge of the arena, and the vast audience, with bowed heads and unhappy hearts, went slowly on their homeward way, mourning greatly that one so young and fair, or so old and respected, should have deserved such a dreadful fate.

But if the accused person opened the other door, there came forth from it a lady, the most suitable to his years and station that his Majesty could select from among his fair subjects; and to this dy he was immediately married, as a reward of his innocence. It mattered not that he might already possess a wife and family, or that his affections might be upon an object of his own selection: the king allowed no such arrangements to interfere with his great scheme of revenge and reward. The exercises, as in the other instance, took place immediately, and in the arena. Another door opened beneath the king, and a priest, followed by a band of choirboys, and dancing maidens blowing joyful airs on golden horns, advanced to where the pair stood side by side; and the wedding was promptly and cheerfully carried out. Then the gay brass bells rang forth, the people shouted happily, and the innocent man, preceded by children scattering flowers on his path, led his bride to his home.

This was the king's method of administering justice. Its perfect fairness is obvious. The criminal could not know out of which door would come the lady: he opened either he pleased, without having the slightest idea whether, in the next instant, he was to be eaten or married. On some occasions the tiger came out of one door, and on some out of the other. The decisions of this tribunal were not only fair, they were definitely determined: the accused person was instantly punished if he found himself guilty; and if innocent, he was rewarded on the spot, whether he liked it or not. There was no escape from the judgments of the king's arena.

The institution was a very popular one. When the people gathered together on one of the great trial-days, they never knew whether they were to witness a bloody death or a gay marriage. This touch of uncertainty lent an interest to the occasion which it could not otherwise have got. Thus the masses were entertained and pleased, and the thinking part of the community could bring no charge of unfairness against this plan; for did not the accused person have the whole matter in his own hands?

This half-barbaric king had a daughter as fair as fair, and with a soul as commanding as his own. As is usual in such cases, she was the apple of his eye, and was loved by him above all humanity. Among his courtiers was a young man of that fineness of blood and lowness of station common to the ordinary heroes of romance who love royal maidens. This royal maiden was well satisfied with her lover, for he was handsome and brave above all others in this kingdom; and she loved him with a strength that had enough of barbarism in it to make it exceedingly warm and strong. This love affair moved on happily for many months, until one day the king happened to discover its existence. He did not hesitate in regard to his duty. The youth was immediately cast into prison, and a day was appointed for his trial in the king's arena. This, of course, was an especially important occasion; and his majesty, as well as all the people, was greatly interested in the workings and development of this trial. Never before had such a case occurred; never before had a subject dared to love the daughter of a king. In after years such things became common enough; but then they were, in no slight degree, unusual and startling.

The tiger-cages of the kingdom were searched for the most savage and cruel beasts, from which the fiercest animal might be selected for the arena; and the ranks of maiden youth and beauty throughout the land were carefully surveyed by proper judges, in order that the young man might have a fitting bride in case fate did not determine for him a different destiny. Of course everybody knew that the deed with which the accused was charged had been done. He had loved the princess, and neither he, she, nor anyone else thought of denying the fact; but the king would not think of allowing any fact of this kind to interfere with the workings of the tribunal, in which he took such a great delight and satisfaction. No matter how the affair turned out, the youth would be disposed of; and the king would take a beautiful pleasure in watching the course of events, which would determine whether or not the young man had done wrong in allowing himself to love the princess.

The appointed day arrived. From far and near the people gathered, and crowded the great arena; and those unable to get in massed themselves against its outside walls. The king and his court were in their places, opposite the two doors—those fateful gates, so terrible in their likeness.

All was ready. The signal was given. A door beneath the royal party opened, and the lover of the princess walked into the arena.

all, beautiful, fair, his appearance was greeted with a low sound of admiration and anxiety. Half the audience had not known so grand a youth had lived among them. No wonder the princess loved him! What a terrible thing for him to be there!

As the youth advanced into the arena, he turned, as the custom was, to bow to the king: but he did not think at all of that royal person; his eyes were fixed upon the princess, who sat to the right of her father. Had it not been for the touch of barbarism in her nature it is probable that lady would not have been there; but her intense soul would not allow her to be absent on an occasion in which she was so terribly interested. From the moment that the order had gone forth that her lover should decide his fate in the king's arena, she had thought of nothing, night or day, but this great event and the various subjects connected with it. With more power, influence and force of character than anyone who had ever before been interested in such a case, she had done what no other person had done—she had possessed herself of the secret of the doors. She knew in which of the two rooms that lay behind those doors stood the cage of the tiger, with its open front, and in which waited the lady. Through these thick doors, heavily curtained with skins on the inside, it was impossible that any noise or suggestion should come from within to the person who should approach to raise the latch of one of them; but gold, and the power of a woman's will, had brought the secret to the princess.

And not only did she know in which room stood the lady ready to come out, all bright and beautiful, should her door be opened, but she knew who the lady was. It was one of the fairest and loveliest of the ladies of the court who had been selected as the reward of the accused youth, should he be proved innocent of the crime of desiring one so far above him; and the princess hated her. Often had she seen, or imagined that she had seen, this fair creature throwing glances of admiration upon the person of her lover, and sometimes she thought these glances were seen and even returned. Now and then she had seen them talking together; it was but for a moment or two, but much can be said in a brief space; it may have been on most unimportant things, but how could she know that?

The girl was lovely, but she had dared to raise her eyes to the loved one of the princess; and, with all the strength of the savage blood given to her through long lines of completely barbaric ancestors, she hated the woman who trembled behind that silent door.

When her lover turned and looked at her, and his eye met hers as she sat there paler and whiter than anyone in the vast ocean of anxious faces about her, he saw, by that power of quick feeling which is given to those whose souls are one, that she knew behind which door crouched the tiger, and behind which stood the lady. He had expected her to know it. He understood her nature, and his soul was assured that she would never rest until she had made plain to herself this thing, hidden to all other lookers-on, even to the king. The only hope for the youth in which there was any element of certainty was based upon the success of the princess in discovering this mystery; and the moment he looked upon her, he saw she had succeeded, as in his soul he knew she would succeed.

Then it was that his quick and anxious glance asked the question, 'Which?' It was as plain to her as if he shouted it from where he stood. There was not an instant to be lost. The question was asked in a flash; it must be answered in another.

Her right arm lay on the cushioned parapet before her. She raised her hand, and made a slight, quick movement toward the right. No one but her lover saw her. Every eye was fixed on the man in the arena.

He turned and with a firm and rapid step he walked across the empty space. Every heart stopped beating, every breath was held, every eye was fixed immovably upon that man. Without the slightest hesitation, he went to the door on the right and opened it.

Now, the point of the story is this: Did the tiger come out of that door, or did the lady?

The more we reflect upon this question the harder it is to answer. It involves a study of the human heart which leads us through various confusions of passion, out of which it is difficult to find our way. Think of it, fair reader, not as if the decision of the question depended upon yourself, but upon that hot-blooded, half-barbaric princess, her soul at a white heat beneath the combined fires of despair and jealousy. She had lost him, but who should have him?

How often, in her waking hours and in her dreams, had she started in wild horror and covered her face with her hands as she thought of her lover opening the door on the other side of which waited the cruel teeth of the tiger!

But how much oftener had she seen him at the other door! How in her dreadful dreams had she torn her hair when she saw his start of delight as he opened the door of the lady! How her soul had burned in agony when she had seen him rush to meet that woman, with her bright cheek and sparkling eye of triumph; when she had seen him lead her forth, his whole frame fresh with the joy of recovered life; when she had heard the glad shouts from the crowds, and the wild ringing of the happy bells; when she had seen the priest, with his joyous followers, advance to the couple and make them man and wife before her very eyes; and when she had seen them walk away together upon their path of flowers followed by the tremendous shouts of the happy people in which her one despairing shriek was lost and drowned!

Would it not be better for him to die at once, and go to wait for her in the blessed regions of a half-barbaric futurity?

And yet, that awful tiger, those shrieks, that blood!

Her decision had been indicated in an instant, but it had been made after days and nights of dreadful deliberation. She had known she would be asked, she had decided what she would answer, and, without the slightest hesitation, she had moved her hand to the right.

The question of her decision is one not to be lightly considered, and it is not for me to presume to set myself up as the one person able to answer it. And so I leave it with all of you: Which came out of the opened door—the lady, or the tiger?

GLOSSARY

The words are defined in the senses in which they are used in the book. The abbreviations used are: (n.) for noun, (v.) for verb, (a.) for adjective, and (Am.) for American.

A

abominable, dreadful.

abrupt, sudden.

absorb in (v.), 1. completely devote to. 2. -ing, taking all one's attention.

absurd, foolish.

academy, school.

accomplice, companion in wrongdoing.

acquittal, being set free in a court of law.

administer, carry on the work of a judge.

afar, far away.

afloat, floating on the water.

agony, great suffering.

ale, bitter drink, like beer, made from grain.

all fours, on hands and knees.

ambush, hiding-place for men who wish to attack by surprise.

ancestors, those persons from whom one is descended.

anticipate, publish before the right time.

anticlimax, sudden end to excitement after a thrilling story.

apple of one's eye, favourite.

apron, piece of cloth worn in front to protect clothes.

arena, central space with seats all round it, used for games or public shows.

arouse, awaken.

asparagus, vegetable whose tops are eaten.

ass, fool.

astern, behind.

attic, room just under the roof of a house.

autograph, person's own handwriting.

B

bacon, salted meat from the back and sides of a pig.

bail (v.), throw water out from a boat.

ballad, short story told in the form of a poem.

bandage (v.), tie a long piece of cloth round a wound.

bang (v.), knock with a loud noise.

bar, place where strong drink is sold; -TENDER, man who looks after bar.

barbaric (a.), without proper laws or customs.

barracks, long building in which soldiers live.

bedlam, place for madmen.

behalf, *in his*, for the purpose of helping him.

biblical (a.), belonging to the Bible, the holy book of the Christians.

blink (v.), close and open the eyes quickly.

blouse (n.), loose outer garment worn by women on upper part of body.

bluff (n.), trick.

bookmaker, one who receives bets.

bored, to be tired.

bounce (v.), jump into the air.

bow (n.), front of a boat.

box a person's ears, strike him on the ears or head.

brave (n.), warrior.

C

casual, careless and unplanned.

catastrophe, event which causes great suffering.

caterpillars, insects with many legs.

cavalry (n.), soldiers on horses.

celery, vegetable stem generally eaten uncooked.

census, counting of the people in a country.

challenge, problem; invitation to face a difficulty.

change, making, paying the toll and receiving the change.

chap, man.

chat, friendly unimportant talk.

chatter, knock together, as with teeth.

chew (v.), break up food with the teeth.

choir, group of singers.

christen (v.), give a name to a person.

chuckle (n.), quiet laugh.

circulate, spread.

civic, having to do with a city.

clam, large shell-fish.

client, one who gets advice from a lawyer.

climax, most exciting of a number of exciting events.

clutch (v.), hold tightly.

coach, person who gives special training.

coast (v.), sail in a ship which visits the ports along the coast.

coconut, large round fruit in a hard shell.

comedy, amusing.

commemorate (v.), make people remember an event by writing of it.

commence, begin.

commonwealth, state.

complexion, colour of the face.

comrade, friend.

concentrate, direct all efforts upon.

consecutive, following in order.

constable, policeman.

contender, competitor.

convent, building for religious women who often teach.

cop, policeman.

corn, ears of, the head of this plant.

coroner, officer of the law who inquires into the causes of sudden death.

corpse, dead body.

corridor, narrow covered way joining two parts of one building.

counter, 1. used to make meanings with the idea of the opposite; 2. long
   table where food is eaten or money paid.

courtier, person who attends at a king's court.

crackle (n.), noise like walking on dry leaves.

craft, boat.

creak (v.), make a sharp high sound (of one thing rubbing on another).

crest, top edge of a wave.

crooked, not straight.

crouch (v.), bend down before jumping.

cultured (a.), educated.

cunning (n.), deceitful skill and knowledge.

cyclone, powerful wind and storm.

cynical (a.), not believing in the goodness of people.

D

daisy, very common small flower.

damn, a swear word.

date, an appointment.

deacon, officer of the church below a priest.

dearth, lack.

deliberate (a.), intentional.

deliberation, thought.

dense (a.), thick.

depot, place where soldiers' stores are kept.

deprive, leave without.

deserter, soldier who runs away from the army.

despite, in spite of.

dessert, sweet dish served at the end of a meal (Am.).

destiny, fate.

detachment, small group of soldiers.

dictate (v.), order.

diet, special food for reasons of health.

dietician, an expert on diets.

diggings (n.), land where people dig for gold.

double-cross (v.), deceive.

doze (v.), be half asleep.

dregs (n.), dirty liquid at the bottom of a drink.

dumb, stupid.

dumpling, round mass of boiled food made of flour, fat, etc.

dwindle (v.), become less and less in number through battle.

E

eat it off, decide the competition by eating until one of them could eat no more.

economy, a wish to save money.

eloquent, moving.

embark (v.), go on to a ship.

emerge (v.), to be seen.

emergency, sudden happening which makes it necessary to act without delay.

emphasis, special force given to certain words so that they will be noticed and remembered; *emphasize,* give this force to words.

engraver, one who cuts names, pictures, etc., on wood.

enterprising (a.), courageous, not afraid to try something new.

enthusiastic (a.), eager and interested.

exaggerate (v.), say something is better than it is.

exhaustion, being at the end of one's strength.

exhibition, display.

exploit, great deed.

F

fall, autumn (Am.).

features, the parts of the face.

fiancee, woman who is promised in marriage.

figure of speech, words not to be understood in their exact meaning.

fin, wing-like part on the back and side of a fish.

fist closed hand.

flask, flat bottle.

foam, mass of bubbles or small round balls of liquid filled with air.

focus (n.), in recognisable detail.

forward (v.), send on to another address.

foul, act which is against the rules.

freckle, light brown spot on the face.

frivolous (a.), not serious.

frontier, new country in which people are beginning to settle.

froth, mass of bubbles or hollow balls of liquid containing air; result of excitement or anger.

furious (a.), angry.

G

gallery, large hall for paintings.

gallop (n.), horse running at its fastest speed.

gang, crowd of men working together.

gazette, newspaper.

gin, colourless strong drink.

ginger-ale, harmless drink.

glare (v.), look fiercely at.

gluttony, habit of eating too much.

Goddam (a.), horrible; exactly 'God curse you'.

gossip, worthless talk about people.

grab, take hold of by force.

gravy, liquid which comes out of cooked meat.

grim, unpleasant.

grin, wide smile.

groceries, food.

growl, make a low angry sound in the throat.

gully, small valley worn by running water.

gunwale, upper edge of the side of a boat.

gutter (n.), channel alongside the road for carrying water away.

gymnastics, throwing and jumping.

H

hint, something said indirectly.

hip, upper part of the leg where it joins the body.

hiss (v.), make a sound like the letter 's'.

hobby, something done just for amusement.

hoof, solid part of a horse's foot; HOOFPRINT, mark made by this on the ground.

hospitality, welcome.

hostile (a.), acting like an enemy.

hue and cry, raising the alarm to get help in catching someone.

hullabaloo, great noise and confusion.

humanity (n.), the human race.
humiliate (v.), make one ashamed.

I

identical (a.), same.
identification, proof to show who one is.
identity, showing who one is.
idiot, fool.
illegal, unlawful.
impartial, just.
impose (v.), lay an unpleasant duty upon a person.
impress (v.), cause to remember.
imprisonment, being put into prison.
impudent -ly, 1. brave(ly), with an air of confidence. 2. rude.
impulse, sudden desire to act.
incident, event.
incorruptible, that cannot be made evil.
indecent, not proper.
indignation, state of anger; INDIGNANT, in this state.
inevitable, that cannot be avoided.
infest (v.), to be full of, ordinarily used in connexion with unpleasant insects.
inlet, small arm of the sea.
intense, serious and thoughtful.
interpreter, one who translates the meaning of speech or events for another.
irresistible, that cannot be resisted.
irritation, annoyance.
item, a piece of news.

J

Jewish, belonging to the Jews, or people whose history is in the first part of the Bible.
jurymen, twelve persons chosen to decide questions of fact in a law court.

K

keep after, continue to talk about.
kid, child or young person.
kidnap (v.), take away a child so as to ask for money for returning him.

L

landlady, woman who gives use of furnished rooms for rent.
landscape, beautiful natural scene.

atch, simple lock for a door.
edge, narrow flat place in a wall.
eech, small water creature that fixes itself tightly to the skin.
egacy (n.), things passed on to us from the past.
egion, army, as in the Foreign Legion of N. Africa.
ife-belt, thing put round the waist to prevent one sinking in water.
ily-livered (a.), cowardly.
imp (a.), not stiff, like a piece of wet cloth.
imp (v.), walk as if with a wounded leg.
iver, inside part of a sheep or cow.
obster, a shell-fish.

M

make out, see.
malaria, a fever found in the hot areas of the earth.
manslaughter, unlawful killing of a person without meaning to kill him.
martyr, one who is put to death for refusing to give up his faith.
masculine, having to do with men.
mash (v.), make into a soft mass.
means, money.
meditate (v.), think deeply.
melancholy (a.), sad.
menu, list of food.
messing about, doing unimportant things.
miracle, the impossible that is possible.
miser, man who saves and loves money.
mob, disorderly crowd of people.
mourners (n.), those who show grief for the dead.
mournful, sad.
movie, film.
mow (v.), cut grass.
muffin, light flat cake eaten hot with butter.
mummy, dead body kept from decay as in ancient Egypt.
mustard, yellow, strong-tasting powder mixed with water and eaten with
  meat.

N

narrative, story.
navigation, art of sailing a ship.
negative, in the, which says this is wrong.
neutral, taking neither side in a contest.
nibble (v.), take little bites of, as a mouse does.
nigger (n.), impolite word for a member of a black race.

oath, take an, promise in the name of God that one will speak the truth.
oats, grain used for horse food.
oblige (v.), help.
obvious, clear.
olive, small, egg-shaped fruit.
on-shore wind, wind that blows from the sea towards the shore.
opponent, person who takes the other side in a contest.
oral (a.), by word of mouth.
orchard, field of fruit trees.
outlaw, one who is put outside the protection of the law.
outrage (v.), shock and make angry.
oversubscribe, pay more money than is necessary.
oyster, flat type of shell-fish.

P

paddle (v.), move a boat with an oar.
pane, sheet of glass.
pants, trousers (Am.).
parapet, small wall in front of a seat.
parental, belonging to parents.
parrot, bird that is able to speak.
part (n.), line from which one's hair is brushed to left or right (Am.).
party, competitor or person.
pasteboard, made of stiff thick paper.
pathos, sadness.
patrolman, policeman.
pedal (v.), move that part of a machine pressed by the feet; e.g., bicycle.
pedlar, one who sells from door to door.
penetrate (v.), enter into.
pepper, hot-tasting powder.
perpendicular, straight up in the air.
persist (v.), continue in.
phony, false.
phosphorescence, small sea-creatures that shine in the dark.
photo-finish, close finish needing to be decided by a photograph; usually in a horse-race.
pirate, one who attacks and steals, usually from ships.
plaster, sticky mixture put on the skin as a medicine.
play the races, bet at the horse-races.
pork, meat from a pig.
port (a.), left side of a boat.
precaution, care taken before an event in order to prevent it happening.

receded by children, with children going in front.

recisely, exactly.

reposterous (a.), foolish or unbelievable.

resume, be bold in behaviour.

rime, best part of one's life.

rivileged, fortunate.

rize-fighter, boxer who fights for a prize of money, professional fighter.

rofound, deep.

romotion, move to a higher rank.

rophet, man who can foretell the future.

ropriety, good behaviour.

rosecution, group that takes action against another in a court of law.

rosperity, wealth.

uff (v.), blow out.

umpkin, very large round yellow fruit.

uppy, young dog.

R

agged, torn.

aid, sudden attack.

ambling, wandering and not easy to follow.

ansack (v.), search thoroughly.

ansom (n.), a sum of money paid to set a prisoner free.

eaction, an act that results from another act.

efined (a.), made better.

efrain (v.), prevent oneself from doing something.

efuge, house of, a building on the coast with stores for shipwrecked sailors.

einforcements, fresh groups of soldiers.

eins, leather bands used in driving a horse.

ely on, depend on.

eservation, part of a country set aside for a special people.

estraint, control.

esurrection, rising again from the dead.

evolver, small gun.

hythmic (a.), with a regular beat.

iddle, puzzle.

ing, place closed in with ropes in which two men box.

oller, very large wave.

omance, fanciful story.

ooming-house, boarding-house.

um, strong drink made from sugar.

umour, common talk, probably untrue.

ustle (n.), a noise as of dead leaves.

salad, uncooked leaves and vegetables.

saloon, place for buying and drinking strong drink.

sandwich, meat, etc., between two pieces of bread.

sausage, meat cut small and put into a pipe-like skin.

scalp, skin of the head.

scar, mark left on the skin by a disease.

scheme, plan.

schooner, sailing ship, usually not very large and having two masts.

scramble (v.), climb, using the hands and knees.

seasoning (n.), being more prepared and ready.

seaward, out of the sea.

sensation, great excitement.

serenely, calmly.

sergeant (n.), rank in the army third from the bottom.

shallows, edge of the sea where it is not deep.

shark, large fish that eats men.

shiver (v.), shake with cold.

shrewd, of keen mind.

shriek, high loud cry.

shrink (v.), become smaller.

simultaneously at one and the same time.

sinister (a.), that threatens evil.

skinny (a.), thin.

skyrocket, one who is loud and difficult in behaviour.

slam (v.), shut with a noise.

slang, words commonly used in speech but not always considered suitab
or correct.

slap (v.), strike with the flat of the hand.

slate, dark grey rock.

sling, piece of leather used for throwing a stone.

sloppy, silly and foolish.

smallpox (n.), dangerous easily spread disease causing spots.

smash (v.), break in pieces.

snack, small quick meal.

so long, goodbye.

soak, thoroughly wet.

sparkle (v.), shine.

spectator, one who watches.

splash (n.), noise similar to that of something falling into water.

splendour, beauty and brightness.

spray, fine drops of water flying through the air.

squire, country gentleman.

take, post driven into the ground.

talk, stem of a plant on which the leaves grow.

tammer (v.), speak with difficulty.

tand-in, one person who will take the place of another.

tarch, fattening substance in foods.

tartle (v.), surprise and frighten.

teak, thick piece of meat.

tern, back end of a boat.

stew (v.), cook in water.

tockade, place surrounded by a wall made of upright posts.

tool, small seat with no back.

torey, first, second, etc., floor of a house.

trawberry, small red fruit.

street-car, tram or car on an electric railway running in the streets of a town.

stuffing, nice-tasting mixture put into a bird before cooking it.

substitute, thing used in place of something else.

subtle (a.), difficult to feel or understand.

subway, underground railway.

sullenly, with ill-temper.

summary, short account of a piece of writing.

summit, the top.

sun-glass, glass that collects the heat of the sun for lighting purposes.

supernatural, more than natural.

surf, broken water where the sea runs up on the land.

swagger (v.), walk or speak in a proud self-satisfied way.

swamp (v.), fill with water and sink.

swede, native of Sweden.

T

talent, skill.

talkative, one who talks much.

tar, black oily liquid obtained from coal and wood.

temporary, lasting a short time.

terms, conditions.

testify (v.), solemnly say from one's own experience.

testimony, a solemn telling of the truth in a law court.

text, words actually used by a writer.

thump, heavy noise.

tinkle (v.), make a sound like a small bell.

tip (n.), a piece of advice on the right horse to bet on.

tiptoe (v.), walk on toes of feet to make little noise.

toad, small ugly jumping creatures living in cool wet places.

toast, piece of bread made brown and hard on the surface by being he
    in front of the fire.
toll, money paid for going along a road.
tongue in his cheek, half-seriously.
torch, small electric hand-light.
torment (n.), great pain.
torture, great suffering.
tragedy, extreme sadness.
tragic (a.), extremely sad.
tramp, walk heavily.
treachery, deceiving act.
tread upon (v.), walk on.
tremendous, great.
tribunal, court of law.
trifle (n.), thing of no importance.
trot (v.), make movement just quicker than walking (of a horse).
trudge (v.), walk as when one is very tired.
tub, wooden container for liquid, though in Am. used for any bath.
turkey, large bird.
twig, thin branch of a tree.
twin, one of two children born at one birth.

U

undernourishment, not enough food.
unfounded, without facts to prove it true.
unique, like no other.
unsubstantial, not solid.
uproar, excitement and noise.

V

vagabond, homeless wanderer.
vague, faint.
vanity, pride.
vegetation, plant life.
verdict, careful final opinion given in a court of law.
vest, waistcoat (Am.).
vice, instrument used for holding wood tightly while one cuts it.
vicinity, surrounding area.
viciousness (n.), badness of a deliberate kind.
vinegar, very sour liquid often used in cooking.
vocal (a.), belonging to the voice.

W

ager, bet.
ay, in rather a bad, quite seriously ill.
edged, to be, to be caught.
hisky, strong drink made from grain.
iggle (v.), move slightly.
retch, bad person.

Y

ankee, an American, in the past especially from the northern states.

Z

est, eagerness.
ither (n.), musical instrument with strings which are sounded by picking them.

THE BRIDGE SERIES
General Editor JA Bright